**napa bulletin 13**

T0307822

# Race, Ethnicity, and Applied Bioanthropology

■ Claire C. Gordon, ed.

National Association for the Practice of Anthropology
A Unit of the American Anthropological Association

NAPA Bulletins are occasional publications of the National Association for the Practice of Anthropology, a Unit of the American Anthropological Assocition.

Pamela Amoss and Ralph J. Bishop
*General Editors*

Library of Congress Cataloging-in-Publication Data

Race, ethnicity, and applied bioanthropology / Claire C. Gordon, editor
p. cm.—(NAPA bulletin ; 13)
Includes bibliographical references.
ISBN 0-913167-59-2
1. Race. 2. Physical anthropology. 3. Applied anthropology.
I. Gordon, Claire C. II. Series.
GN269.R33 1993
573—dc20 93-35791
CIP



ISBN 0-913167-59-2

# Contents

# Introduction

## Why Classify Race?

Claire C. Gordon

Why, when many contemporary anthropologists are abandoning racial concepts, do we devote an entire publication to the subject? The crux of this apparent paradox lies squarely in differing expectations of the classificatory process.

Criticisms of racial classification advanced in a popular introductory textbook indicate some of the expectations and concomitant disappointments that biological anthropologists have with race: no racial groups are discrete in the sense that they differ in all traits from one another; racial boundaries based upon one set of traits may not be consistent with those derived from another set; most classification schemes are consistent with neither current nor past population structures; and despite decades of intense research, the "experts" still disagree on both categories and criteria for racial classification (Nelson and Jurmain 1991). In short, an *acceptable* racial classification is expected to be typological, phylogenetic, consistent with contemporary human population structures, and appropriate for all avenues of research. With expectations such as these, is it any wonder that racial classification is the subject of intense disappointment?

Indeed, as recently pointed out in the American Anthropological Association's proposed revisions to the UNESCO (1964) "Document on Biological Aspects of Race," typological classificatory systems cannot properly represent all aspects of human variation, and when the complex interactions between genetics, environment, and behavior are poorly understood, racial typologies permit (if not promote) social abuse and discrimination. However, not all classification is typological in nature. This publication assumes a broader definition of "racial" classification and explores applied settings in which the appropriate units of analysis are not just nontypological: they may, to a considerable extent, be defined solely by the problem at hand.

As practicing biological anthropologists, how do we escape the dilemmas surrounding racial classification that have led many of our colleagues to recommend abandoning the term *race* altogether? The definition of race provided in Nelson and Jurmain's textbook offers considerable insight into both the source and solution to the "racial dilemma":

> **Race** Currently defined by anthropologists as a breeding population; formerly applied to a group of people who resembled each other in physical appearance. Many anthropologists do not believe the term to be a useful one when applied to humans. [Nelson and Jurmain 1991:608]

It is not surprising that traditional definitions of race focused on morphological similarity, whereas contemporary definitions focus on breeding populations, the unit of evolutionary change. The shift in focus from a descriptive, comparative "old" biological anthropology to a problem-oriented, evolutionary "new" biological anthropology has placed new and extensive demands on the information conveyed by classificatory systems. In addition to grouping individuals that are alike in their physical attributes, classifications are now also expected to reflect evolutionary relationships.

The problems created by demanding that classificatory systems imply evolutionary relationships are certainly not unique to anthropology. Biologists reviewing the fields of morphometry and taxonomy note that evolutionary theory can actually inhibit studies of morphological variation by slaving empirical classifications of form to phylogenetic systematics (Reyment et al. 1984; Sneath and Sokal 1973). One solution to this problem is to draw a clear distinction between phenetic classifications, which imply only similarity, and phylogenetic classifications, which imply evolutionary relationships. From Sneath and Sokal's point of view, the description and classification of empirically observed variation is best conducted independently from, and prior to, the generation of evolutionary hypotheses.

When classificatory systems are divorced from evolutionary theory and phylogenetic systematics, they can serve as *tools* for scientific investigation rather than ends in themselves, thus avoiding many traditional objections to human racial classification. Classifications, for example, can be problem-oriented rather than absolute. Criteria and groupings can, and sometimes should, be entirely different in evolutionary, biomedical, forensic, and engineering applications. Individual groups need not be reproductively isolated from one another; indeed, it is appropriate to recognize that some traits have clinal distributions across groups, thus leading to classifications that are probabilistic, not typological.

Obviously, problem-oriented classifications permit only limited inference—something that may be difficult for scientists to communicate to the general public. The more specific a classification's purpose, the narrower will be the range of inferences that can be drawn from the information contained in that classification (Sneath and Sokal 1973). Certainly from that point of view, the fusion of phenetic and phylogenetic classification within an evolutionary paradigm is a highly desirable goal. However, failure to attain such a lofty goal in the case of *Homo sapiens* is not necessarily sufficient reason for anthropologists to stop classifying human physical variation altogether. Perhaps the only relevant question in this regard is raised within Nelson and Jurmain's definition of race: is racial classification useful?

The criterion of usefulness is particularly meaningful to applied or "practicing" bioanthropologists, and a symposium to address this issue was co-sponsored by the National Association for the Practice of Anthropology and the Biological Anthropology Section of the American Anthropological Association (AAA). The symposium, "Race, Ethnicity, and Applied Bioanthropology," was held at the 90th Annual Meeting of the AAA, on November 20, 1991, in Chicago. This publication is comprised of all but two of the articles presented in that symposium, and includes an additional article by Alice Brues that was also presented at the 90th annual meetings.

As the articles to follow indicate, *problem-oriented* population classifications are not only useful, but they may also be necessary to successful work in the applied fields of human engineering and forensic anthropology. Specialists in human engineering utilize anthropometric and biomechanic data to ensure that materiel systems such as protective clothing, machinery, workstations, automobiles, and aircraft are designed to safely accommodate the wide variety of body sizes and shapes in the consumer population for whom the systems are intended. Forensic specialists utilize dental, osteological, and anthropometric data to aid in the identification of unknown individuals. Both applications rely heavily on knowledge of racial/ethnic diversity in physical characteristics. In forensics, racial/ethnic classifications are used to narrow the field of potential matches for an unknown individual. In human engineering, racial/ethnic classifications are used to identify and summarize anthropometric data separately for population subgroups that have body size and shape distributions significantly different from the general consumer population.

As indicated in Robert Walker's opening, most body dimensions differ significantly among American racial/ethnic groups, and failure to identify and address the engineering needs of unique populations could result in disproportionate disaccommodation of minority groups—such as Asians, Hispanics, and Native Americans—in military clothing and equipment design. Public transportation systems and military/industrial protective equipment and workstations that fail to accommodate the anthropometric distributions of unique subgroups potentially compromise their safety and well-being. Even commercial systems such as fashion clothing and luxury cars must address anthropometric variation in their markets. To do so efficiently requires identification and summarization of data for demographic subgroups that may be defined by race, ethnicity, age, and gender.

The need for classifications such as race also arises in the application of secular trend models to estimate the future anthropometric distributions of consumers. As Gordon and Greiner point out, consumer groups are usually composed of individuals from multiple biological subpopulations, each of which may be undergoing its own secular trend. Further, the factors influencing participation in a consumer group such as the U.S. Army may variably influence selection from among biologically and culturally defined subpopulations, and these too may change independently over time. In this application, racial, ethnic, and gender classifications are needed to model anthropometric change in culturally and biologically heterogenous consumer groups. The structure and level of detail needed in such classifications may be situational, relating directly to the biological and cultural mechanisms influencing anthropometric change in the consumer population.

The interface between biologically defined race and ethnicity terminology needed for human engineering application and public perceptions of these terms is addressed by Gordon and Bell. Their results indicate that the army's three minority groups, Hispanics, Asians, and Native Americans, are underestimated by as much as 50 percent in official records *primarily* due to poor terminology definition, the presence and overuse of "Other" categories in the classification system, and probable reluctance to discuss a "socially sensitive" subject with recruits, even when the accuracy of such information clearly benefits them. Significantly, the same "socially sensitive" subject avoided by many army recruiters received enthusiastic responses from most U.S. Army Anthropometric Survey subjects when explained within a human engineering context (Walker, n.d.). Furthermore, when the relationships between racial and ethnic classifications and population affiliation were explicitly defined and properly explained, virtually all subjects identified as "Other" in official army records could select a specific population affiliation.

The following chapter by Madeleine Hinkes provides a much needed overview of the practical aspects of racial classification and identification in forensic anthropology. She notes that whereas classical racial archetypes are unrealistic, multiple clinally distributed skeletal traits can be successfully used to identify unknown individuals with one of five primary racial groups, despite the fluid nature of variation across these group "boundaries." This paradox is echoed by Rhine and Schneider: although forensic anthropologists recognize (indeed exploit) the multivariate and clinal nature of human skeletal variation, their success as part of the overall medicolegal process depends upon making a single "archetypal" racial identification that is based upon a classification system that is *geographically relevant* and *locally understood* by law enforcement officials. The issues this paradox fosters when a synthesis of forensic methods and evolutionary biology is desired are discussed at length by Sauer at the end of this publication.

The need for geographically relevant classification systems in forensic anthropology is demonstrated in some detail by Rhine's review of skeletal variation among contemporary populations from the American Southwest. His article also reinforces the need for multivariate approaches to classification criteria, particularly in the case of admixed populations such as American Hispanics. Schneider expands Rhine's ideas to include population-specific dental variation, which may be the only evidence available when remains have undergone severe trauma or postmortem degradation.

Once again, problem-oriented flexibility in classification systems is required. Whereas Rhine may rarely need to distinguish between Native Americans and Asians, Schneider, who works with Vietnam war casualties, must do so frequently.

Lest we lose sight of our role in the larger social and academic communities, the final two articles in this publication address the relationships between applied racial classifications, public perceptions of race, and academic racial theory. Alice Brues's commentary on racial classifications and public perception draws a sharp distinction between political definitions/inferences about race and biological reality. She notes that denial of visible racial variability merely damages our professional credibility and promotes ignorance and suggests, instead, that we base our racial terminology and discussions firmly in the biological realm of individual and population variation and educate the public to their meaning.

Norman Sauer's article addresses racial concepts in the academic realm: that is, when we utilize broad-brush racial classifications such as those devised by Linnaeus, do we do justice to what contemporary anthropologists know about human population variation? Indeed, when such broad classifications are utilized in academic research, do they sometimes inhibit investigations of biological phenomena? Sauer concludes that while useful in certain applied contexts, most racial classifications are too broad to capture the population variation needed for research in anthropology and epidemiology. Ironically, Sauer's conclusion echoes a theme running throughout this publication that some readers may find disturbing: classification of human biological variation is truly problem oriented; there is no single "right" answer.

As is apparent from the earlier articles, specialists in both human engineering and forensics must address race and ethnic variation in their work. In conjunction with sex and age, racial and ethnic affiliations are among the most important characteristics for forensic identification. In fact, skeletal and dental markers of population affiliation are becoming increasingly important in mass disaster identification as international travel becomes more commonplace. The growth of a multinational global community also affects the importance of racial/ethnic variation in human engineering as materiel systems are designed more often for multinational marketing. Even in domestic markets, the U.S. population is so biologically heterogenous that racial/ethnic variation in body size and shape must be explicitly considered at every phase of the development and testing process to ensure that all relevant consumer subgroups are adequately accommodated.

Applied anthropologists have a social and professional responsibility not to walk away from tough problems when their expertise can aid in a solution. As is pointed out by several contributors, medical examiners and engineers will proceed with or without the expertise of anthropologists. If racial and ethnic classifications improve the probability that unknown remains can be identified and can increase anthropometric compatibility in engineering designs, then research to refine these problem-oriented classification systems should receive high priority in applied bioanthropology.

## References Cited


Nelson, H., and R. Jurmain
1991 Introduction to Physical Anthropology. 5th ed. St. Paul, MN: West Publishing Company.

Reyment, R. A., R. E. Blackith, and N. A. Campbell
1984 Multivariate Morphometrics, 2nd ed. New York: Academic Press.

Sneath, P. H. A., and R. R. Sokal
1973 Numerical Taxonomy. San Francisco, CA: W. H. Freeman and Company.

UNESCO
1964 UNESCO Statement on Biological Aspects of Race. Position paper adopted at the UNESCO Moscow Conference, August 18, 1964.

Walker, R. A.
n.d. "1988 U.S. Army Anthropometric Survey: Daily Field Operations" and "1988 U.S. Army Anthropometric Survey: Self-Reported Race and Ethnicity." Behavioral Sciences Division, U.S. Army Natick R,D,& E Center, Natick, MA, unpublished manuscripts.

# Race, Ethnicity, and Human Engineering

## The Impact of Racial Variation on Human Engineering Design Criteria

Robert A. Walker

Most variation in anthropometric dimensions among different groups occurs in two domains: body size and body proportion. A large number of differences in anthropometric dimensions between males and females are due to differences in body size. Compounding these differences between males and females are those differences in size and proportion due to race. *Homo sapiens* is a continuously variable species, and the boundaries between racial groups are not hard and fast. Because of this continuous variation of human physical traits, the definition of human races becomes problematic (Garn 1971; Leach 1975; Roberts 1953, 1978; Sauer 1991; Schreider 1950; Singh et al. 1977; Sokal and Uyttershaut 1987; Sunderland 1975). Racial variation must, however, be dealt with because differences in body size and shape clearly exist among various human groups. Both overall size and body weight are clinally distributed, with lower body weights and smaller stature being more frequent in tropical or equatorial regions, and heavier body weights and greater stature being more frequent at higher latitudes in accordance with biogeographical rules (Pianka 1983; Roberts 1978). These differences are reflected in human populations of diverse geographic origins (Garn 1971; Roberts 1978). Because these differences exist, it is important to know the racial and gender composition of a design's target population. Thus, in order to avoid disaccommodation of specific groups, there exists a need for racial classification for purposes of design.

### Materials and Methods

The practical result of these body proportion and body size variants is that such differences must be accommodated in the design and development of clothing and equipment. From August 1987 to July 1988, the U.S. Army Natick Research, Development, and Engineering Center undertook a large-scale anthropometric survey for this purpose. During the course of this survey, 132 directly measured anthropometric dimensions were gathered for each subject. The three-dimensional coordinates of another 26 head and face landmarks were collected for these same individuals utilizing an automated headboard device (Annis and Gordon 1988; Gordon et al. 1989). A total of 164 anthropometric dimensions were included in this analysis, including all 132 directly measured body dimensions, as well as 32 head and face dimensions derived from the automated three-dimensional headboard coordinates (Annis and Gordon 1988; Clauser et al. 1988). A complete listing of the measurements included in this analysis is given in the appendix. Definitions of all dimensions and landmarks used as a part of this survey are presented elsewhere (Clauser et al. 1988).

Subjects participating in the 1988 U.S. Army Anthropometric Survey were selected by a sampling strategy designed to ensure that all racial groups were well represented and that both men and women were sampled in adequate numbers. Dimensions included in this data base were measured in the same manner by the same anthropometrists for both men and women. Therefore, the data are amenable to simultaneous comparison on the basis of both race and gender. The 1988 U.S. Army Anthropometric Survey data base is unique in this regard among large-scale anthropometric surveys conducted upon U.S. military personnel.

Participants in the 1988 U.S. Army Anthropometric Survey were asked to identify their own racial backgrounds and that of their parents on a biographical questionnaire. Participants were also interviewed with regard to their ethnic identification. Final racial categorization of subjects was arrived at from the racial identifications reported by subjects and the ethnic identities that were the result of interviews with the subjects.

The study sample (see Table 1) was restricted to individuals from one of five primary groups: white, black, Hispanic, Asian/Pacific, and Native American. This analysis does not include soldiers of mixed race for two reasons. First, mixed-race soldiers comprise a relatively small portion of the total army population. Second, this is a very heterogeneous category. Mixed-race soldiers represent a variety of racial/ethnic backgrounds that may not constitute any single biological population or ancestry.

In order to test the simultaneous effects of race and gender upon the values of anthropometric dimensions, a series of two-way ANOVAS with interaction using gender and race as the main effects were performed (Sokal and Rohlf 1981). In this context, two-way analysis of variance tests whether or not men and women of different racial groups differ from one another in

**Table 1**
**Gender and Racial Composition of the Study Sample**

| | White | Black | Hispanic | Asian | Native American | Total |
|---|---|---|---|---|---|---|
| Male | 1,643 | 1,507 | 1,054 | 446 | 86 | 4,736 |
| Female | 1,425 | 1,405 | 341 | 139 | 48 | 3,358 |
| Total | 3,068 | 2,912 | 1,395 | 585 | 134 | 8,094 |

the mean values for each of the 164 dimensions examined. Because 164 dimensions are examined, the Type I error for each test was set at 0.03 percent. This allows a 0.03 percent chance of obtaining a spurious but significant difference between race-gender cells. This 0.03 percent significance level allows an overall experimentwise error rate of 5 percent when the test is run for all 164 dimensions. Therefore, the chance of finding a spurious significant difference among the race-gender groups for any of the variables does not exceed 5 percent (Sokal and Rohlf 1981).

When results of the analyses of variance indicate that significant race and gender effects exist, it is then necessary to isolate which race-gender groups differ specifically from one another. Such differences were identified with post hoc tests for significant differences among means. The method used in this analysis was Scheffe's Test (Scheffe 1959). The Scheffe method is applicable to groups of unequal sample sizes and is suitable for any post hoc comparisons because there is no requirement that the post hoc comparisons be independent.

## Results

The 164 dimensions examined are comprised of 116 body dimensions and 48 head and face dimensions (16 directly measured and 32 measured with the automated headboard device). Of the 48 head and face dimensions examined, 24 exhibited significant race/gender interaction. Similarly, 18 of the 116 body dimensions exhibited significant race/gender interaction. Thus, of the total 164 dimensions examined, 42 (or 36.2 percent) exhibited significant race/gender interaction. For those 42 dimensions that exhibited significant race/gender interaction terms, a series of one-way analyses of variance were performed that examine the effects of race upon anthropometric dimensions within each gender.

Race and gender individually demonstrate significant effects on almost all dimensions. There are, however, three exceptions. Axillary arm circumference and abdominal extension depth (sitting) do not exhibit significant racial differences, while crotch length (posterior at natural indentation) does not exhibit a significant difference due to gender. The remaining 161 dimensions all exhibit significant differences due to gender and race.

After the significance of the main effects had been assessed by means of analyses of variance, the significance of the differences among individual group means were examined using Scheffe's test for post hoc comparisons. Because of the large number of dimensions examined, only a sample of dimensions that demonstrate typical intergroup differences are discussed in detail. Complete results of these analyses are presented in an army technical report (Gordon and Walker 1993). In the results summarized below, the following group designations apply: white females (WF), black females (BF), Hispanic females (HF), Asian females (AF), Native American females (NF), white males (WM), black males (BM), Hispanic males (HM),

Asian males (AM), and Native American males (NM). Each asterisk indicates a significant difference between the two indicated groups at an experimentwise error rate of five percent.

For most dimensions in this study, all males, regardless of geographic population, are larger than all females. There are some exceptions, of course, particularly with regard to head and face dimensions. For some dimensions, females of some groups—especially black, Asian, and Native American—demonstrate broader facial dimensions than males of other racial groups. Biocular breadth, maximum, is a good example (see Table 2).

Other results of Scheffe's tests demonstrate that whites tend to be significantly larger in dimensions related to trunk length and most trunk circumferences than other groups. Vertical trunk circumference and cervicale height, sitting, demonstrate this point (see Tables 3 and 4). Likewise, blacks tend to exhibit smaller trunk breadths and depths than other groups (see Tables 5 and 6), and greater limb and limb segment lengths (see Tables 7 and 8) as with, for example, radiale-stylion length and trochanterion height.

Interestingly, Native Americans tend to differ significantly less frequently from whites in measurements related to trunk lengths and circumferences than do blacks, while they differ less frequently from blacks in measurements related to limb and limb segment lengths than they do whites. Hispanics and Asians tend to differ more frequently from the other three groups than they do from each other. This is probably a reflection of their smaller size for most dimensions.

As noted above, there are further interesting patterns of differences among head and face dimensions, which are reflected in the results of Scheffe's tests. Blacks and whites demonstrate greater head length and head circumference than other groups, while Asians demonstrate the greatest head breadths (see Table 9).

These differences are largely a result of the greater size in general of whites and blacks. There are, however, differences in specific dimensions that can be cited. Whites have the narrowest faces (see Table 10), as demonstrated by biinfraorbitale breadth and bitragion breadth, and the most protuberant noses (see Table 11). Blacks demonstrate the greatest interpupillary breadths and biinfraorbitale breadths (see Table 12), while Asians and Native Americans demonstrate the greatest bizygomatic breadths (see Table 13).

Because of the very large sample sizes, many statistically significant differences were of small magnitude. While indeed these differences are real, from a design perspective many of them may be negligible. One means of determining which of these differences are of functional importance is to look at a comparison of percentile values. Traditionally, requirements for military systems specify that items must accommodate the 5th through 95th percentile range of the user population for a specific variable or set of variables. In the case of the army, these ranges most often apply to percentile distributions for the general active duty army population,

**Table 2**
**Race/Gender Variation in Biocular Breadth, Maximum (mm)**

| Mean | Group | WF | HF | WM | BF | HM | AF | NF | BM | NM | AM |
|---|---|---|---|---|---|---|---|---|---|---|---|
| 117.32 | WF | | | | | | | | | | |
| 119.67 | HF | * | | | | | | | | | |
| 120.39 | WM | * | | | | | | | | | |
| 122.11 | BF | * | * | * | | | | | | | |
| 122.40 | HM | * | * | * | | | | | | | |
| 122.43 | AF | * | | | | | | | | | |
| 123.16 | NF | * | | | | | | | | | |
| 124.39 | BM | * | * | * | * | * | | | | | |
| 124.59 | NM | * | * | * | | | | | | | |
| 125.54 | AM | * | * | * | * | * | * | | | | |

**Table 3**
**Race/Gender Variation in Cervicale Height, Sitting (mm)**

| Mean | Group | BF | HF | AF | NF | BM | WF | HM | AM | NM | WM |
|---|---|---|---|---|---|---|---|---|---|---|---|
| 614.7 | BF | | | | | | | | | | |
| 620.0 | HF | | | | | | | | | | |
| 624.4 | AF | | | | | | | | | | |
| 632.6 | NF | | | | | | | | | | |
| 641.1 | BM | * | * | * | | | | | | | |
| 654.4 | WF | * | * | * | | * | | | | | |
| 663.8 | HM | * | * | * | * | * | * | | | | |
| 664.8 | AM | * | * | * | * | * | * | | | | |
| 676.3 | NM | * | * | * | * | * | * | | | | |
| 684.7 | WM | * | * | * | * | * | * | * | * | | |

**Table 4**
**Race/Gender Variation in Vertical Trunk Circumference (mm)**

| Mean | Group | AF | BF | HF | NF | BM | AM | WF | HM | NM | WM |
|---|---|---|---|---|---|---|---|---|---|---|---|
| 1468.3 | AF | | | | | | | | | | |
| 1469.3 | BF | | | | | | | | | | |
| 1473.5 | HF | | | | | | | | | | |
| 1497.0 | NF | | | | | | | | | | |
| 1504.7 | BM | * | * | * | | | | | | | |
| 1558.6 | AM | * | * | * | * | * | | | | | |
| 1559.3 | WF | * | * | * | * | * | | | | | |
| 1569.5 | HM | * | * | * | * | * | | | | | |
| 1588.5 | NM | * | * | * | * | * | | | | | |
| 1599.1 | WM | * | * | * | * | * | * | * | * | | |

### Table 5
### Race/Gender Variation in Bispinous Breadth (mm)

| Mean | Group | BF | BM | HF | WF | AF | HM | AM | WM | NF | NM |
|---|---|---|---|---|---|---|---|---|---|---|---|
| 208.9 | BF | | | | | | | | | | |
| 218.6 | BM | * | | | | | | | | | |
| 224.5 | HF | * | | | | | | | | | |
| 228.0 | WF | * | * | | | | | | | | |
| 231.2 | AF | * | * | | | | | | | | |
| 232.6 | HM | * | * | * | * | | | | | | |
| 235.0 | AM | * | * | * | * | | | | | | |
| 235.7 | WM | * | * | * | * | | | | | | |
| 239.9 | NF | * | * | | | | | | | | |
| 240.5 | NM | * | * | * | * | | | | | | |

### Table 6
### Race/Gender Variation in Chest Depth (mm)

| Mean | Group | AF | AM | BF | BM | WF | HF | WM | HM | NF | NM |
|---|---|---|---|---|---|---|---|---|---|---|---|
| 230.7 | AF | | | | | | | | | | |
| 234.3 | AM | | | | | | | | | | |
| 238.4 | BF | | | | | | | | | | |
| 239.1 | BM | | | | | | | | | | |
| 239.5 | WF | | | | | | | | | | |
| 241.6 | HF | | | | | | | | | | |
| 243.5 | WM | * | * | * | * | | | | | | |
| 243.9 | HM | * | * | * | * | | | | | | |
| 246.7 | NF | | | | | | | | | | |

### Table 7
### Race/Gender Variation in Radiale-Stylion Length (mm)

| Mean | Group | AF | HF | WF | NF | BF | AM | HM | WM | NM | BM |
|---|---|---|---|---|---|---|---|---|---|---|---|
| 231.0 | AF | | | | | | | | | | |
| 235.1 | HF | | | | | | | | | | |
| 237.1 | WF | | | | | | | | | | |
| 239.4 | NF | | | | | | | | | | |
| 252.4 | BF | * | * | * | * | | | | | | |
| 256.2 | AM | * | * | * | * | | | | | | |
| 261.4 | HM | * | * | * | * | * | * | | | | |
| 267.2 | WM | * | * | * | * | * | * | * | | | |
| 269.7 | NM | * | * | * | * | * | * | | | | |
| 280.0 | BM | * | * | * | * | * | * | * | * | | |

**Table 8**
**Race/Gender Variation in Trochanterion Height (mm)**

| Mean | Group | AF | HM | WF | NF | AM | BF | HM | NM | WM | BM |
|---|---|---|---|---|---|---|---|---|---|---|---|
| 811.3 | AF | | | | | | | | | | |
| 832.1 | HM | | | | | | | | | | |
| 851.3 | WF | * | * | | | | | | | | |
| 851.4 | NF | | | | | | | | | | |
| 872.0 | AM | * | * | * | | | | | | | |
| 878.2 | BF | * | * | * | | | | | | | |
| 896.8 | HM | * | * | * | * | * | * | | | | |
| 923.9 | NM | * | * | * | * | * | * | | | | |
| 924.8 | WM | * | * | * | * | * | * | * | | | |
| 950.4 | BM | * | * | * | * | * | * | | | * | |

**Table 9**
**Race/Gender Variation in Head Breadth (mm)**

| Mean | Group | WF | BF | HF | NF | AF | BM | WM | HM | NM | AM |
|---|---|---|---|---|---|---|---|---|---|---|---|
| 144.2 | WF | | | | | | | | | | |
| 144.3 | BF | | | | | | | | | | |
| 145.5 | HF | | | | | | | | | | |
| 148.1 | NF | | | | | | | | | | |
| 150.0 | AF | * | * | * | | | | | | | |
| 151.3 | BM | * | * | * | | | | | | | |
| 151.3 | WM | * | * | * | * | * | * | * | | | |
| 152.8 | HM | * | * | * | * | * | * | | | | |
| 153.5 | NM | * | * | * | * | | | | | | |
| 155.8 | AM | * | * | * | * | * | * | * | * | | |

**Table 10**
**Race/Gender Variation in Biinfraorbitale Breadth (mm)**

| Mean | Group | WF | HF | AF | NF | WM | HM | NM | AM | BF | BM |
|---|---|---|---|---|---|---|---|---|---|---|---|
| 65.08 | WF | | | | | | | | | | |
| 66.44 | HF | | | | | | | | | | |
| 66.56 | AF | | | | | | | | | | |
| 66.56 | NF | | | | | | | | | | |
| 67.00 | WM | * | | | | | | | | | |
| 67.98 | HM | * | | | | | | | | | |
| 68.18 | NM | * | | | | | | | | | |
| 68.90 | AM | * | * | | | * | | | | | |
| 70.06 | BF | * | * | * | | * | * | | | | |
| 72.26 | BM | * | * | * | * | * | * | * | * | * | |

**Table 11**
**Race/Gender Variation in Bitragion Breadth (mm)**

| Mean | Group | WF | HF | BF | NF | AF | WM | BM | HM | AM | NM |
|---|---|---|---|---|---|---|---|---|---|---|---|
| 135.06 | WF | | | | | | | | | | |
| 137.33 | HF | * | | | | | | | | | |
| 137.55 | BF | * | | | | | | | | | |
| 140.36 | NF | * | | | | | | | | | |
| 140.89 | AF | * | * | * | | | | | | | |
| 144.17 | WM | * | * | * | | * | | | | | |
| 145.01 | BM | * | * | * | | * | | | | | |
| 146.12 | HM | * | * | * | * | * | * | | | | |
| 148.98 | AM | * | * | * | * | * | * | * | * | | |
| 149.51 | NM | * | * | * | * | * | * | * | | | |

**Table 12**
**Race/Gender Variation in Nose Protrusion (mm)**

| Mean | Group | AF | BF | AM | BM | HF | NF | HM | NM | WF | WM |
|---|---|---|---|---|---|---|---|---|---|---|---|
| 16.84 | AF | | | | | | | | | | |
| 16.99 | BF | | | | | | | | | | |
| 17.12 | AM | | | | | | | | | | |
| 17.31 | BM | | | | | | | | | | |
| 17.85 | HF | | * | | | | | | | | |
| 17.90 | NF | | | | | | | | | | |
| 18.26 | HM | * | * | * | * | | | | | | |
| 18.40 | NM | | * | | | | | | | | |
| 19.24 | WF | * | * | * | * | * | | * | | | |
| 19.30 | WM | * | * | * | * | * | | * | | | |

**Table 13**
**Race/Gender Variation in Interpupillary Breadth (mm)**

| Mean | Group | WF | HF | AF | NF | WM | BF | HM | AM | NM | BM |
|---|---|---|---|---|---|---|---|---|---|---|---|
| 60.4 | WF | | | | | | | | | | |
| 61.6 | HF | * | | | | | | | | | |
| 62.4 | AF | * | | | | | | | | | |
| 62.8 | NF | | | | | | | | | | |
| 63.4 | WM | * | * | | | | | | | | |
| 64.5 | BF | * | * | * | | * | | | | | |
| 64.6 | HM | * | * | * | | * | | | | | |
| 64.9 | AM | * | * | * | | * | | | | | |
| 64.9 | NM | * | * | * | | | | | | | |
| 67.4 | BM | * | * | * | * | * | * | * | * | * | |

**Table 14**
**Race/Gender Variation in Bizygomatic Breadth (mm)**

| Mean | Group | WF | BF | HF | NF | AF | WM | BM | HM | NM | AM |
|---|---|---|---|---|---|---|---|---|---|---|---|
| 130.2 | WF | | | | | | | | | | |
| 132.2 | BF | * | | | | | | | | | |
| 132.3 | HF | * | | | | | | | | | |
| 136.2 | NF | * | | | | | | | | | |
| 137.5 | AF | * | * | * | | | | | | | |
| 139.6 | WM | * | * | * | | | | | | | |
| 141.1 | BM | * | * | * | * | * | * | | | | |
| 141.5 | HM | * | * | * | * | * | * | | | | |
| 144.8 | NM | * | * | * | * | * | * | * | * | | |
| 145.8 | AM | * | * | * | * | * | * | * | * | | |

which may have relatively few individuals from such population groups as Asians and Native Americans (see Table 15).

As a result, some racial groups may have little impact on armywide anthropometric distributions, and when their body dimensions also differ significantly from the "majority" racial groups, materiel system requirements may disproportionately disaccomodate them.

To assess the rates of disaccommodation for specific groups, the percentage of individuals in these groups falling above and below the overall army male and female 5th and 95th percentile values for specific dimensions were examined. For both males and females, Hispanics and Asians are excessively disaccommodated by the overall army 5th percentile values. More than 10 percent of Hispanic females fall under the 5th percentile value in 57 of the 164 dimensions studied, while more than 10 percent of Asian females fall under the 5th percentile value for fully 84 dimensions. For white, black, and Native American females, the comparable figures are 0, 3, and 15 of 164 dimensions respectively. Among males, the comparable figures for Hispanics and Asians are, respectively, 49 and 96 of 164 dimensions examined. These results are detailed in Table 16.

The rates of disaccommodation at the lower end of the size range appear to be due to basic differences in body size. Hispanics and Asians are, in general, considerably smaller than the other three groups examined. For example, Hispanics and Asians are overrepresented in the lower ranges for such key size-related dimensions as stature (see Table 17), span (see Table 18), and weight (see Table 19).

When head and face dimensions are examined, however, the overrepresentation of Hispanics and Asians in the lower ranges of the values disappear. Here, under- and overrepresentation of specific groups in the lower range of sizes is much more unpredictable. In the head and face, it appears that there is much greater variation in shape than in size. Here again, the pattern is similar for both males and females.

**Table 15**
**Gender-Specific Racial Composition of the U.S. Army, 1988**

| | White | Black | Hispanic | Asian | Native American | Other |
|---|---|---|---|---|---|---|
| Males | 66.2% | 25.9 | 3.9 | 1.5 | .5 | 2.0 |
| Females | 51.7 | 41.8 | 2.6 | 1.4 | .6 | 1.9 |

*Source*: Gordon et al. 1989.

**Table 16**
**Number of Dimensions for Which 10 Percent or More Individuals Are Smaller Than the Overall Army 5th Percentile Value**

| | White | Black | Hispanic | Asian | Native American |
|---|---|---|---|---|---|
| Male | 0 | 25 | 49 | 96 | 13 |
| Female | 0 | 3 | 57 | 84 | 15 |

**Table 17**
**Race/Gender Variation in Stature (mm)**

| Mean | Group | AF | HF | NF | BF | WF | AM | HM | NM | BM | WM |
|---|---|---|---|---|---|---|---|---|---|---|---|
| 1576.5 | AF | | | | | | | | | | |
| 1587.6 | HF | | | | | | | | | | |
| 1615.8 | NF | | | | | | | | | | |
| 1629.9 | BF | * | * | | | | | | | | |
| 1632.4 | WF | * | * | | | | | | | | |
| 1689.2 | AM | * | * | * | * | * | | | | | |
| 1708.2 | HM | * | * | * | * | * | | | | | |
| 1747.8 | NM | * | * | * | * | * | * | | | | |
| 1755.8 | BM | * | * | * | * | * | * | * | | | |
| 1761.8 | WM | * | * | * | * | * | * | * | | | |

The examination of race-specific variation at the upper end of the size range reveals a considerably different pattern, as would be expected from the known differences in the distribution of body sizes and proportions among different human groups. Again, however, the patterns that emerge are similar among both females and males.

At the upper end of the size range, the groups most likely to be accommodated fully are whites and Hispanics. There is not a single dimension for which more than 10 percent of white females or males exceed the 95th per-

**Table 18**
**Race/Gender Variation in Span (mm)**

| Mean | Group | AF | HF | WF | NF | BF | AM | HM | WM | NM | BM |
|---|---|---|---|---|---|---|---|---|---|---|---|
| 1603.0 | AF | | | | | | | | | | |
| 1625.2 | HF | | | | | | | | | | |
| 1645.3 | WF | * | | | | | | | | | |
| 1665.0 | NF | | | | | | | | | | |
| 1709.2 | BF | * | * | * | | | | | | | |
| 1746.4 | AM | * | * | * | * | * | | | | | |
| 1772.2 | HM | * | * | * | * | * | * | | | | |
| 1813.0 | WM | * | * | * | * | * | * | * | | | |
| 1818.0 | NM | * | * | * | * | * | * | | | | |
| 1864.1 | BM | * | * | * | * | * | * | * | * | | |

**Table 19**
**Race/Gender Variation in Weight (kg)**

| Mean | Group | AF | HF | WF | BF | NF | AM | HM | NM | WM | BM |
|---|---|---|---|---|---|---|---|---|---|---|---|
| 58.05 | AF | | | | | | | | | | |
| 59.01 | HF | | | | | | | | | | |
| 61.67 | WF | | | | | | | | | | |
| 62.36 | BF | | | | | | | | | | |
| 62.39 | NF | | | | | | | | | | |
| 73.11 | AM | * | * | * | * | * | | | | | |
| 45.16 | HM | * | * | * | * | * | | | | | |
| 77.45 | NM | * | * | * | * | * | | | | | |
| 78.36 | WM | * | * | * | * | * | * | | | | |
| 78.59 | BM | * | * | * | * | * | * | | | | |

centile value. For Hispanic males, this occurs for only two dimensions (both are head and face dimensions), and for Hispanic females, this occurs only once (hand length).

The groups most disaccommodated at the upper end of the size range are blacks, Asians, and Native Americans. Among females, 10 percent or more blacks fall above the 95th percentile for 13 dimensions. For Asian females, this figure is 17, while for female Native Americans, this figure is 52 of 164 dimensions. The comparable figures for black, Asian, and Native American males are 30, 13, and 20 of 164 dimensions respectively. This information is summarized in Table 20.

Furthermore, the reasons for the rates of disaccommodation at the upper end of the size ranges are different from those at the lower end. As stated previously, the rates of disaccommodation at the lower end appear to be due primarily to general differences in body size among racial groups. At the upper end, the differences appear to be due primarily to differences

**Table 20**
**Number of Dimensions for Which 10 Percent or More Individuals Exceed the Overall U.S. Army 95th Percentile Value**

| | White | Black | Hispanic | Asian | Native American |
|---|---|---|---|---|---|
| Male | 0 | 30 | 1 | 13 | 20 |
| Female | 0 | 13 | 1 | 17 | 52 |

in proportion and shape among groups, rather than to general body size differences. The majority of the dimensions for which more than 10 percent of any given group exceed the general army 95th percentile are head and face dimensions, especially among blacks, Asians, and Native Americans. Additionally, among blacks more than 10 percent exceed the general army 95th percentile for most dimensions related to general body linearity (e.g., buttock-knee length, buttock-popliteal length, forearm-hand length, functional leg length, gluteal furrow height, lateral femoral epicondyle height, trochanterion height, among others).

## Discussion and Conclusions

It is well established that *Homo sapiens* is a highly variable species. As this analysis has demonstrated, anthropometric differences among racial groups, while perhaps small in magnitude, certainly must be accounted for in the establishment of criteria for ergonomic design. For some applications, such as the design and development of protective masks, accommodating these differences could be the difference between life and death.

With an increasingly more diverse population in the United States and other nations, accommodation of such biological diversity in design criteria is essential. Simply accommodating a specific range of sizes for the general population can disaccommodate large portions of specific subgroups within the general population. Among multiracial societies such as the United States, this could pose an especially vexing problem. Certainly in the future, as the racial composition of the United States and other large nations undergoes changes, greater emphasis will have to be given to the design and ergonomic needs of specific subgroups of the general population, both in military and civilian applications.

The results of this analysis emphasize the need for and purpose of racial classification when considering design criteria. If important differences among these different human groups are ignored, then large portions of certain groups will be ill served by standard design criteria.

## References Cited

Annis, J. F., and C. C. Gordon
1988 The Development and Validation of an Automated Headboard Device for Measurement of Three-Dimensional Coordinates of the Head and Face. Technical Report NATICK/TR-88/048. Natick, MA: U.S. Army Natick Research, Development, and Engineering Center.

Clauser, C., I. Tebbetts, B. Bradtmiller, J. McConville, and C. C. Gordon
1988 Measurer's Handbook: U.S. Army Anthropometric Survey, 1987–1988. Technical Report NATICK/TR-88/043. Natick, MA: U.S. Army Natick Research, Development, and Engineering Center.

Garn, S. M.
1971 Human Races. 3rd ed. Springfield, IL: Thomas.

Gordon, C. C., and R. A. Walker
1993 Gender and Race Variation in U.S. Army Anthropometry: Univariate Studies. Technical Report NATICK/TR-93/***. Natick, MA: U.S. Army Natick Research, Development, and Engineering Center.

Gordon, C. C., B. Bradtmiller, T. Churchill, C. E. Clauser, J. T. McConville, I. Tebbetts, and R. A. Walker
1989 1988 Anthropometric Survey of U.S. Army Personnel: Methods and Summary Statistics. Technical Report NATICK/TR-89/044. Natick, MA: U.S. Army Natick Research, Development, and Engineering Center.

Leach, E. R.
1975 Cultural Components in the Concept of Race. *In* Racial Variation in Man. F. J. Eblin, ed. Pp. 27–54. Oxford: Blackwell Scientific Publications.

Pianka, E. R.
1983 Evolutionary Ecology. 3rd ed. New York: Harper and Row.

Roberts, D. F.
1953 Body Weights, Race, and Climate. American Journal of Physical Anthropology 11:533–558.
1978 Climate and Human Variability. 2nd ed. Menlo Park, CA: Cummings.

Sauer, N. J.
1991 The Concept of Race in Applied Anthropology: A Legacy of Linneaus. Paper presented at the 1991 Annual Meeting of the American Anthropological Association, Chicago.

Scheffe, H.
1959 The Analysis of Variance. New York: Wiley.

Schreider, E.
1950 Geographical Distribution of the Body-Weight/Body-Surface Ratio. Nature 165:286.

Singh, I. P., M. K. Bhasin, and S. L. Malik
1977 Anthropometric Variables in Indian Population—An Environmental Perspective. Symposia Biologica Hungarica 20:123–131.

Sokal, R. R., and F. J. Rohlf
1981 Biometry. 2nd ed. San Francisco, CA: Freeman.

Sokal, R. R., and Uyttershaut, H.
1987 Cranial Variation in European Populations: A Spatial Autocorrelation Study at Three Time Periods. American Journal of Physical Anthropology 74:21–38.

Sunderland, E.
1975 Biological Components of the Races of Man. *In* Racial Variation in Man. Pp. 9–25. Oxford: Blackwell Scientific Publications.

## Appendix
## Anthropometric Dimensions Analyzed*

1. Abdominal extension depth, sitting
2. Acromial height
3. Acromial height, sitting
4. Acromion-radiale length
5. Ankle circumference
6. Axilla height
7. Axillary arm circumference
8. Ball of foot circumference
9. Ball of foot length
10. Biacromial breadth
11. Biceps circumference, flexed
12. Bideltoid breadth
13. Bimalleolar breadth
14. Bispinous breadth
15. Bitragion chin arc
16. Bitragion coronal arc
17. Bitragion crinion arc
18. Bitragion frontal arc
19. Bitragion submandibular arc
20. Bitragion subnasale arc
21. Bizygomatic breadth
22. Bustpt/thelion-bustpt/thelion brdth
23. Buttock circumference
24. Buttock depth
25. Buttock height
26. Buttock-knee length
27. Buttock-popliteal length
28. Calf circumference
29. Calf height
30. Cervicale height
31. Cervicale height, sitting
32. Chest breadth
33. Chest circumference
34. Chest circumference at scye
35. Chest circumference below breast
36. Chest depth
37. Chest height
38. Crotch height
39. Crotch length (NI)
40. Crotch length (OM)
41. Crotch length, posterior (NI)
83. Overhead fingertip reach
84. Overhead fingertip reach, extended
85. Overhead fingertip reach, sitting
86. Popliteal height
87. Radiale-stylion length

42. Crotch length, posterior (OM)
43. Ear breadth
44. Ear length
45. Ear length above tragion
46. Ear protrusion
47. Elbow circumference
48. Elbow rest height
49. Eye height, sitting
50. Foot breadth, horizontal
51. Foot length
52. Forearm circumference, flexed
53. Forearm breadth
54. Forearm hand length
55. Functional leg length
56. Gluteal furrow height
57. Hand breadth
58. Hand circumference
59. Hand length
60. Head breadth
61. Head circumference
62. Head length
63. Heel-ankle circumference
64. Heel breadth
65. Hip breadth
66. Hip breadth, sitting
67. Iliocristale height
68. Interpupillary breadth
69. Interscye I
70. Interscye II
71. Knee circumference
72. Knee height, midpatella
73. Knee height, sitting
74. Lateral femoral epicondyle height
75. Lateral malleolus height
76. Lower thigh circumference
77. Menton-sellion length
78. Midshoulder height, sitting
79. Neck-bustpoint/thelion length
80. Neck circumference
81. Neck circumference, base
82. Neck height, lateral
124. Waist
125. Wrist-center of grip length
126. Wrist circumference
127. Wrist height
128. Wrist height, sitting

*Extensive definitions given in Clauser et al. 1988; numbers correspond to those in Gordon et al. 1989.

88. Scye circumference
89. Scye depth
90. Shoulder circumference
91. Shoulder-elbow length
92. Shoulder length
93. Sitting height
94. Sleeve length: spine-elbow
95. Sleeve length: spine-scye
96. Sleeve length: spine-wrist
97. Sleeve outseam
98. Span
99. Stature
100. Strap length
101. Suprasternale height
102. Tenth rib height
103. Thigh circumference
104. Thigh clearance
105. Thumb breadth
106. Thumbtip reach
107. Trochanterion height
108. Vertical trunk circumference (ASCC)
109. Vertical trunk circumference (USA)
110. Waist back length (NI)
111. Waist back length (OM)
112. Waist breadth
113. Waist circumference (NI)
114. Waist circumference (OM)
115. Waist depth
116. Waist front length (NI)
117. Waist front length (OM)
118. Waist height (NI)
119. Waist height (OM)
120. Waist height, sitting (NI)
121. Waist height, sitting (OM)
122. Waist hip length
123. Waist (NI)-waist (OM) length
129. Wrist-index finger length
130. Wrist-thumbtip length
131. Wrist-wall length
132. Wrist-wall length, extended

H1. Alare-back of head
H2. Alare-top of head
H3. Bigonial breadth
H4. Biinfraorbitale breadth
H5. Biocular breadth, maximum
H6. Bitragion breadth
H7. Bizygomatic breadth
H8. Cheilion-back of head
H9. Cheilion-top of head
H14. Ectoorbitale-back of head
H15. Ectoorbitale-top of head
H16. Frontotemporale-back of head
H17. Frontotemporale-top of head
H20. Gonion-back of head
H21. Gonion-top of head
H22. Infraorbitale-back of head
H23. Infraorbitale-top of head
H24. Lip length
H25. Maximum frontal breadth
H27. Menton-crinion length
H28. Menton-sellion length
H29. Menton-subnasale length
H31. Minimum frontal breadth
H32. Nose breadth
H33. Nose protrusion
H41. Subnasale-sellion length
H43. Tragion-back of head
H44. Tragion-top of head
H45. Zygion-back of head
H46. Zygion-top of head
H47. Zygofrontale-back of head
H48. Zygofrontale-top of head

# Biocultural Influences in the Analysis of Secular Trends

Claire C. Gordon and Thomas M. Greiner

In a human-engineering setting, anthropometric data collection and statistical analyses focus on target populations—the aggregates of persons who will utilize a particular materiel system or design. Because designs may be in use for several decades after their introduction, secular trends in the anthropometric distributions of target populations are of great concern to the human-factors engineer. These target populations are formed primarily through cultural processes that sample individuals from "parent" biological populations. Unlike many biological populations, temporal analyses of target populations lack an a priori basis for assuming biocultural continuity. To develop applied secular-trend models, it is thus necessary to work around this limitation. One approach to this process will be illustrated by constructing secular-trend models for the target population of the U.S. Army.

### Secular-Trends Models

Secular trends are frequently viewed as biological responses to a changing environment. Improved socioeconomic status, for example, is generally associated with better health care and nutrition, and greater attainment of genetic potential for growth. Herein lies the more traditional realm of secular-trends analysis. Only biological populations undergo secular change as a direct response to a changing environment. However, secular changes in biological parent populations can influence the anthropometric distributions of engineering target populations. Thus, secular trends observed in the army will be due, in part, to secular trends in the U.S. population.

Target populations are built through the actions of culturally determined sampling processes, or "cultural filters," which determine population membership. Thus, secular trends of target populations may be modeled as the interaction of cultural and biological processes (see Figure 1) that change parent populations and influence their relative contribution to the target population. Army cultural filters include the effects of recruiting strategies, entrance requirements, and various societal opinions regarding the merits of military service. Cultural filters, however, can also change over time. This change might be expressed as a change in recruiting strategies

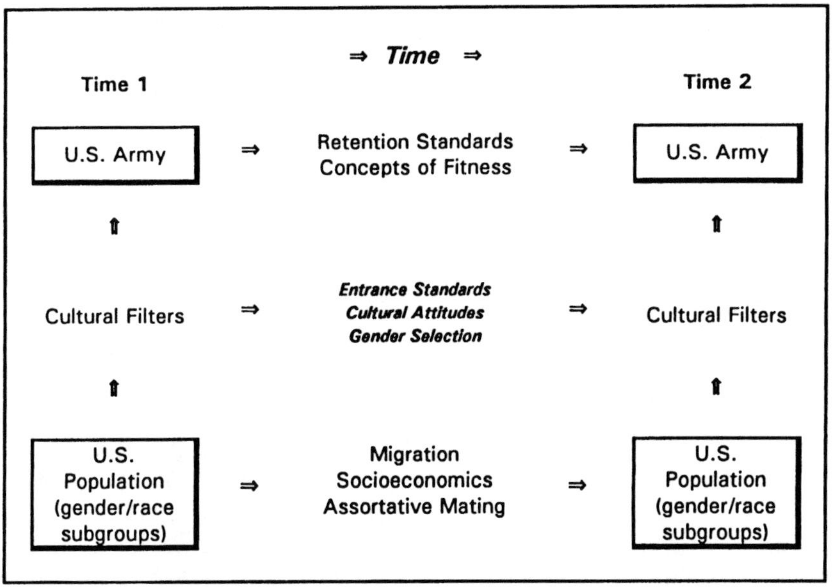


Figure 1. A model of U.S. Army secular trend influences.

as related to racial/ethnic groups, a change in entrance requirements, or a change in the cultural "image" of the soldier (Flegal et al. 1988a, 1988b; Greiner and Gordon 1992). In this way, secular trends in a target population can result from changes in how the target population is created, apart from any secular trends that may be occurring in the parent populations.

Traditional secular-trend models assume biocultural continuity over time. In the applied setting, this assumption must also be justified for the projected future. The operation of a cultural filter creates a complication in that target populations usually do not fulfill this requirement. This complication can be mitigated through identification and separate modeling of target population subsets that more closely meet the assumption of biocultural continuity. The identification of these subsets, however, requires a detailed look at the cultural filters operating in the formation of the target population (see Table 1).

Changes in the anthropometric requirements for admittance into the army can directly influence anthropometric change over time. However, an examination of army regulations (AR40-501) from 1968 to 1989 shows that there has been very little change in the army's anthropometric standards during the period modeled in this study. Therefore, this source of change can be dismissed as being inconsequential.

A variety of cultural filters might act in concert to alter the demographic composition of the army and thus indirectly influence anthropometric

**Table 1**
**Filters Influencing Migration of Civilians into the Army**

1. Anthropometric Requirements
2. Differential Recruiting
   a. Gender
   b. Racial/ethnic group
   c. Age
3. Secondary Factors
   a. Economic status and incentives
   b. Educational requirements for military jobs
   c. Entrance exam scores

change over time. A combination of overt military recruiting strategies and covert cultural opinions can effect change through differential selection by sex, racial/ethnic group, and age. The effects of this type of selection can be addressed in secular-trend studies by dividing the survey data into appropriate demographic subgroups and modeling each separately. Changes in selection criteria for sex, race/ethnicity, and age can then be incorporated in secular-trend models by viewing the target population as a composite of these parts and utilizing weighted estimates.

A third type of cultural filter might be selection on a cultural factor operating within demographic subgroups that correlates with, but is not directly related to, anthropometric dimensions. One example of this might be preferential selection by level of education. Education levels are often related to socioeconomic status, which in turn is associated with a host of biological variables that influence anthropometric distributions (Flegal et al. 1988a, 1998b; Garn et al. 1977; Harlan et al. 1988). The strength of these types of associations, however, varies across cultural groups (Flegal et al. 1988a, 1988b; Meredith 1976). In any case, educational data are not routinely available for army anthropometric survey subjects. Thus, only general trends of educational selection can be discussed. Other cultural criteria might also be at work that have no measurable surrogate. The action of the cultural filter in this fashion can therefore not be controlled or anticipated, and this constitutes a primary limitation in all applied secular-trend models.

## Analytical Methods

Each survey represents a snapshot of anthropometric variation within the army population (see Table 2). To link these data sets, individuals are grouped into cohorts that represent five-year birth intervals. Following procedures outlined by Greiner and Gordon (1992), the mean value for each body dimension is calculated for each cohort. These values are then ad-

**Table 2**
**Birth Year Cohorts and Subjects' Ages by Survey Year**

| | | Subjects' Ages When Measured | | | |
|---|---|---|---|---|---|
| Cohort | Birth Years | 1946 Survey | 1966 Survey | 1977 Survey | 1988 Survey |
| 1 | 1885–89 | 57 | | | |
| 2 | 1890–94 | 52–56 | | | |
| 3 | 1895–99 | 47–51 | | | |
| 4 | 1900–04 | 42–46 | 62 | | |
| 5 | 1905–09 | 37–41 | 57–61 | | |
| 6 | 1910–14 | 32–36 | 52–56 | | |
| 7 | 1915–19 | 27–31 | 47–51 | 58 | |
| 8 | 1920–24 | 22–26 | 42–46 | 53–57 | |
| 9 | 1925–29 | 21 | 37–41 | 48–52 | 59 |
| 10 | 1930–34 | | 32–36 | 43–47 | 54–58 |
| 11 | 1935–39 | | 27–31 | 38–42 | 49–53 |
| 12 | 1940–44 | | 22–26 | 33–37 | 44–48 |
| 13 | 1945–49 | | 17–21 | 28–32 | 39–43 |
| 14 | 1950–54 | | 16 | 23–27 | 34–38 |
| 15 | 1955–59 | | | 18–22 | 29–33 |
| 16 | 1960–64 | | | 17 | 24–28 |
| 17 | 1965–69 | | | | 19–23 |
| 18 | 1970–74 | | | | 18 |

justed for age-related change and submitted to regression analysis. To accommodate very large differences in sample sizes, each cohort's mean value can be weighted by cohort size in the statistical analyses.

These variate regressions produce the following generic equation:

$$AAV = a\,C + b$$

In this linear equation, $b$ is the y-intercept constant and $a$ is the slope of the line. Because this equation describes the relationship between cohort ($C$) and an age-adjusted anthropometric dimension (AAV), the term $a$ is the rate of secular change per five-year period.

While a longitudinal perspective for secular-trend analyses can be obtained by linking the data from two or more anthropometric surveys, their measuring techniques must be carefully scrutinized. Only dimensions measured through strictly comparable techniques can provide data for the analysis. In addition, the definition of population subgroups must be comparable. Furthermore, all relevant birth years must be broadly represented in the available data. When these restrictions are applied to U.S. Army data bases, their combination permits a male analysis comprised of four racial/ethnic groups (whites, blacks, Hispanics, and Asian/Pacific Islanders)

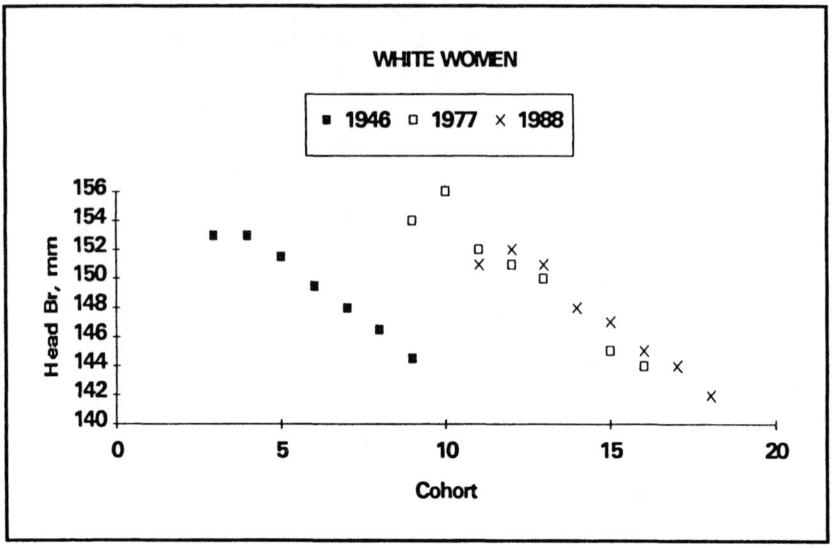


Figure 2. Head breadth (mm) by birth-year cohort.

and a female analysis of only two racial/ethnic groups (whites and blacks). When insufficient data limit modeling to only some segments of the target population, this clearly induces some limitations to the application of results. However, in this case because whites and blacks together comprise 93.4 percent of the females in the army (Gordon et al. 1989), this limitation may not be too serious.

## Temporal Stability of Secular-Trends Models

The crux of secular-trend analysis lies with the construction of reliable and temporally stable models for each of the identified target population subgroups. An important aspect of this is the review and specification of any temporally unstable cultural influences. A parallel examination of estimated secular trends in U.S. Army males and females provides an example of the differential operation of cultural filters and their relative influence on model reliability.

Three major surveys of army women are available to build secular-trend models. However, when these data are plotted against birth-year cohort, there is a consistent separation of the 1946 data set, most dramatically seen in Figure 2: a scatterplot of head breadth versus birth-year cohort. The special nature of several factors operating on the 1946 army women may explain this separation. First, the bulk of these women experienced their growth years during the Great Depression of the 1930s. Inasmuch as economic environment influences growth, these women might be expected to

**Table 3**
**Recent Milestones for U.S. Army Women**

| | |
|---|---|
| 1967 | Public Law 90-130 removes career restrictions and lifts 2 percent cap on women's participation in the military |
| 1972 | End of the military draft and beginning of the All Volunteer Force |
| 1973 | Military women given dependency benefits |
| 1974 | Public Law 93-290 ends age differential for women's enlistment |
| 1975 | End of involuntary discharge for pregnancy |
| 1976 | Women admitted to military academies |
| 1978 | Women's Army Corps abolished |

show unusual anthropometric values relative to other cohorts (Bock and Sykes 1989). Second, the women in the 1946 data set represent the formation of the Women's Army Corps in response to the national emergency of World War II (WWII). As an event, WWII represents a complex, unique, and discontinuous cultural filter whose direct and indirect influences on anthropometric values are difficult to discern. There are insufficient data to "correct" for the unique influence that WWII had on army women's anthropometric distributions. Therefore, the only alternative is to acknowledge that the 1946 survey data represent a separate target population that cannot, at this time, be linked to the later surveys in a larger trend model. Ongoing research in this area will attempt to identify social and demographic differences between the WWII-era Women's Army Corps, their civilian counterparts, and their military "descendants."

While analysis of the remaining two data sets (1977 and 1988) results in more stable secular-trend models, their lack of time depth may limit model reliability. The 1977 and 1988 surveys overlap for all but two birth-year cohorts. Therefore, these data do not provide long-term information on how cultural processes might be affecting the population. Nevertheless, changes in the cultural filters affecting army women might be associated with events between 1967 and 1978 (see Table 3).

In effect, between 1967 and 1978, there was a broadening of the cultural selection criteria that influenced women's participation in the army. These changes may have indirectly influenced anthropometric dimensions even though no specific change in anthropometric selection criteria occurred. It is difficult to delineate indirect cause and effect relationships between cultural actions and anthropometric trend. However, if it could be shown that new cultural filters bring about a shift in the socioeconomic origins of women recruits, then inclusion of socioeconomic level, or some proxy for it, may be needed to enhance model reliability. One possible measure that might be used is the association of socioeconomic level with levels of education. During the period of 1967 to 1978, for example, acceptable levels of education were broadened and entrance levels were lowered for women recruits. However, these changes did not palpably affect the distribution of women's education levels (Soldier Support Center 1982; U.S. Army Military Personnel Center 1977). Therefore, education (even if it were a useful proxy for socioeconomic level) may not be useful in explaining the secular trends of army women.

Because the original 1946 survey data for men are not available, the 1966 and 1988 surveys of army men have been used to build secular-trend models (Greiner and Gordon 1990, 1992). The most important event that might have influenced the cultural filter of male target populations during the last 30 years was the end of the military draft and the beginning of the All Volunteer Force in 1972. Associated with this change, there was a slight decrease in the representation of whites and Hispanics and a slight increase in the representation of blacks and Asians (Gordon et al. 1989; White and Churchill 1971). Cultural filters that act primarily through differential selection, however, are easily controlled through the separate examination of each racial/ethnic group.

There has been some speculation that the shift to an all volunteer army might have indirectly induced a change in the socioeconomic background of recruits. As was the case with women, available source data indicate that there has been very little change in the proportion of high school graduates

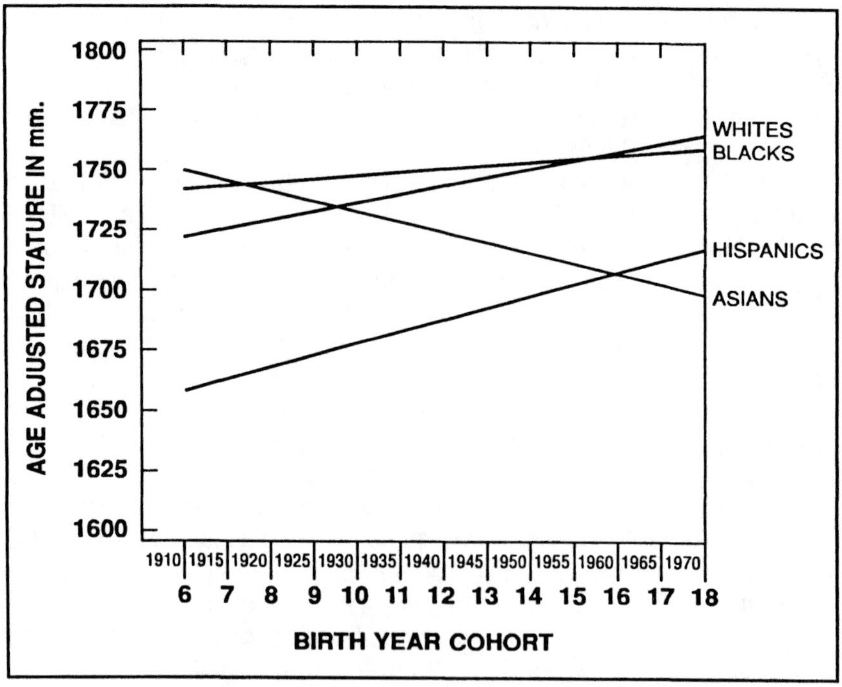


Figure 3. Secular trends of U.S. Army males

within the army, despite an overt shift in recruiting goals in 1979 to target high school graduates (Hunter and Nelson 1982; Soldier Support Center 1982; White and Hosek 1982). Thus, shift in educational level would not seem to be an important influence in the secular trends of army males.

More specific cultural influences may be acting in the case of Asian/Pacific Islander males. From 1966 to 1988 there was a significant increase in the number of foreign-born members of this group, causing a shift from predominately American-born soldiers to predominantly foreign-born solders, most of whom came from the Philippines (Greiner and Gordon 1992). The impact of this shift on stature trends in the U.S. Army Asian/Pacific subgroup is readily seen in Figure 3 and illustrates a classic case in which the available racial/ethnic classification is at too broad a level to provide stable estimates of future stature trends in this subgroup. To improve these estimates, population-specific data and models may be required for such heterogenous groups as Asian/Pacific Islanders, Hispanics, and Native Americans. As indicated below, application of such models requires specific estimates of future minority group frequencies, and as Robert Walker has pointed out, their contribution to the army population is so small that they may have little impact on armywide parameter estimates regardless of the accuracy of their individual secular-trend models.

## Model Applications

Models resulting from cultural filter research and subgroup identifications operate by separately predicting values by birth-year cohort for each demographic subgroup. These models assume biocultural continuity within each of the demographic subgroups. Estimates for future target populations are built by combining individual estimates for each subgroup, weighted by appropriate demographic proportions. In this way, population predictions change according to their demographic makeup. An example of this can be seen by predicting the mean values for stature of army males in the year 2023 (see Table 4).

In this example, there are differences in the trend rates for all identified racial/ethnic groups. When these values are used to predict stature for four target populations with different demographic compositions, the influence of age and racial/ethnic differences become apparent. For stature, increasing the proportion of minority racial/ethnic groups at the expense of whites influences projection values more than would a decrease in average age. This shows that it is important for projections to consider not only rates of change for individual dimensions, but also how the cultural filter might change to alter the demographic composition of the future target population.

In addition to cultural filter considerations, the application of secular-trend models often requires differentiation between statistically significant change and "design"-significant change. Trends that are not statistically

**Table 4**
**Secular Trends in U.S. Army Male Stature**

| Racial/Ethnic Group | Trend (mm/cohort) |
|---|---|
| Whites | 3.71 |
| Blacks | 1.46 |
| Hispanics | 5.34 |
| Asian Pacific Islanders | –5.64 |

| Year | Population[a] | Mean Stature |
|---|---|---|
| 1988 | Current Population | 1756 mm |
| 2023 | No Demographic Change | 1778 mm |
| 2023 | More Minorities | 1770 mm |
| 2023 | Younger Population | 1779 mm |
| 2023 | Younger Population and More Minorities | 1772 mm |

[a]Race/cohort frequencies for each hypothetical population are given in Greiner and Gordon 1990.

significant are unlikely to warrant the redesign of clothing or equipment. However, when trends are statistically significant, they may or may not be significant to engineering design. The engineering significance of a trend depends upon the nature of the design. A statistically significant trend that is small in magnitude may not be important to a design that incorporates a wide-fit tolerance. It is possible, however, for significant but seemingly inconsequential trends to greatly influence equipment that must fit close to

**Table 5**
**Secular Trends in Male Head Dimensions (mm/5 yr cohort)**

| | Breadth | Length | Circumference |
|---|---|---|---|
| Whites | –0.25 | 0.51 | 0.52 |
| Blacks[a] | –0.17 | 0.03 | 0.54 |
| Hispanics[a] | –0.18 | 0.79 | 1.69 |
| Asians[a] | –0.14 | 0.89 | 2.11 |
| Observer Error | 2 mm | 2 mm | 5 mm |

[a]Rates of change are not significantly different among these groups for head breadth; all other race differences are statistically significant at the .05 level or better.

**Table 6**
**Accommodation Projections for an Army Helmet[a]**

| No Demographic Change | | |
|---|---|---|
| Size | 1988 | 2023 |
| Small | 9.9 | 6.0 |
| Medium | 33.7 | 21.3 |
| Large | 40.7 | 30.2 |
| X-large | 13.1 | 10.6 |
| No Fit | 2.7 | 32.0 |

| More Younger Cohorts | | |
|---|---|---|
| Size | 1988 | 2023 |
| Small | 10.4 | 4.7 |
| Medium | 34.2 | 21.8 |
| Large | 43.0 | 31.1 |
| X-large | 11.4 | 9.8 |
| No Fit | 1.0 | 32.6 |

| More Minority Groups | | |
|---|---|---|
| Size | 1988 | 2023 |
| Small | 9.6 | 5.7 |
| Medium | 33.1 | 20.9 |
| Large | 42.1 | 29.9 |
| X-large | 13.2 | 10.8 |
| No Fit | 2.9 | 32.7 |

| More Minorities and Younger Cohorts | | |
|---|---|---|
| Size | 1988 | 2023 |
| Small | 12.9 | 6.3 |
| Medium | 34.6 | 19.6 |
| Large | 38.7 | 29.6 |
| X-large | 11.2 | 12.1 |
| No Fit | 2.5 | 32.5 |

[a]Race/cohort frequencies for each hypothetical population are given in Greiner and Gordon 1990.

the body. An example of this can be seen in the application of the trend models to a close-fitting combat helmet design.

The helmet system used as an example here employs a combination of three head dimensions to determine fit into a four-size system. The secular rates of change for each of these dimensions are small (see Table 5). In fact, the differences between racial groups are smaller than expected observer error rates for these dimensions. Yet, when these small trends are applied to target populations 35 years in the future, the predicted changes in head dimensions greatly influence helmet accommodations (see Table 6). With no demographic change, we would expect to see the mean value of head breadth to decrease by 1.6 mm, head length to increase by 3 mm and head circumference by 4 mm. Two of these changes are still below the allowable observer error. Yet, these small changes are so influential that the current design could conceivably fail to accommodate 32 percent of the target population. Thus, even unspectacular rates of change can interact with close-fitting designs and greatly influence the accommodation of future target populations.

## Conclusions

Applied secular-trend models are rarely built from data gathered with the aim of model construction. However, the application of secular-trend models does not require that all sources of change be identified and understood. Instead, their application relies upon the assumption that past trends will continue into the future. Because this assumption will eventually prove false for any population, it is important to understand a model's limitations before it is applied. An understanding of the mechanisms that contribute to secular trends merely provides some ability to anticipate the sources of instability in the model. Once secular trends are modeled, however, their relevance to design can only be determined by the sensitivity of the design criteria.

## References Cited

Bock, R. D., and R. C. Sykes
1989 Evidence for Continuing Secular Increase in Height Within Families in the United States. American Journal of Human Biology 1:143–148.
Flegal, K. M., W. R. Harlan, and J. R. Landis
1988a Secular Trends in Body Mass Index and Skinfold Thickness with Socioeconomic Factors in Young Adult Men. American Journal of Clinical Nutrition 48:544–551.
1988b Secular Trends in Body Mass Index and Skinfold Thickness with Socioeconomic Factors in Young Adult Women. American Journal of Clinical Nutrition 48:535–543.
Garn, S. M., S. M. Bailey, P. E. Cole, and I. T. T. Higgins
1977 Level of Education, Level of Income, and Level of Fatness in Adults. American Journal of Clinical Nutrition 30:721–725.
Gordon, C. C., T. Churchill, C. E. Clauser, B. Bradtmiller, J. T. McConville, I. Tebbetts, and R. A. Walker
1989 1988 Anthropometric Survey of U.S. Army Personnel: Methods and Summary Statistics. NATICK/TR-89/044. Natick, MA: U.S. Army Natick Research, Development and Engineering Center.
Greiner, T. M., and C. C. Gordon
1990 An Assessment of Long-Term Changes in Anthropometric Dimensions: Secular Trends of U.S. Army Males. NATICK/TR-91/006. Natick, MA: U.S. Army Natick Research, Development and Engineering Center.
1992 Secular Trends of 22 Body Dimensions in Four Racial/Cultural Groups of American Males. American Journal of Human Biology 4(2):235–246.
Harlan, W. R., et al.
1988 Secular Trends in Body Mass in the United States, 1960–1980. American Journal of Physical Anthropology 31:111–116.
Hunter, R.W., and G. R. Nelson
1982 Eight Years with the All-Volunteer Armed Forces: Assessments and Prospects. *In* Military Service in the United States. B. Scowcroft, ed. Pp. 80–128. Englewood Cliffs, NJ: Prentice-Hall.
Laubach, L. L., J. T. McConville, E. Churchill, and R. M. White
1977 Anthropometry of Women of the US Army—1977; Report No. 2, The Basic Univariate Statistics. Technical Report NATICK/TR-77/029. Natick, MA: U.S. Army Natick Research and Development Command.
Meredith, H. V.
1976 Findings from Asia, Australia, Europe, and North America on Secular Change in Mean Height of Children, Youths, and Young Adults. American Journal of Physical Anthropology 44:315–326.
Randall, F. E., and E. H. Munro
1949 Reference Anthropometry of Army Women. Environmental Protection Service Report No. 149. Lawrence, MA: US Army Quartermaster Climatic Research Laboratory.
Soldier Support Center
1982 Army Personnel Composite as of 28 February 1982. ATZI-NCR Report No. 82-1-5. Alexandria, VA: Soldier Support Center.
U.S. Army Military Personnel Center
1977 Army Personnel Composite as of 30 November 1977. DAPC-MSF Report No. 77-35-5. Alexandria, VA: U.S. Army Military Personnel Center

White, J. P., and J. R. Hosek
1982 The Analysis of Military Manpower Issues. *In* Military Service in the United States. B. Scowcroft, ed. Pp. 40–79. Englewood Cliffs, NJ: Prentice-Hall.
White, R. M., and E. Churchill
1971 The Body Size of Soldiers: US Army Anthropometry—1966. Technical Report 72-51-CE. Natick, MA: U.S. Army Quartermaster Research and Engineering Center.

## Problems of Racial and Ethnic Self-Identification and Classification

Claire C. Gordon and Nancy A. Bell

Racial and ethnic classification is a fundamental research tool in applied bioanthropology. In human-factors engineering, for example, these classifications specify groups that differ significantly in their body size and shape distributions. Stratified sampling is then used to ensure that materiel design and testing are done with samples representative of a design's user population. Racial classification also aids identification of minority groups at risk for poor fit even when designs are engineered and tested using representative samples. Racial and ethnic classification in forensic anthropology focuses on groups that differ quantitatively or qualitatively in one or several physical traits that may be observed in the skeleton, dentition, or other remains. These data are then employed in narrowing the pool of potential matches for an unknown individual. In epidemiological research, racial and ethnic classifications specify groups that share common biological and/or cultural features thought to influence disease risk. In application, epidemiological data reported by racial and ethnic group are then used to select high-risk populations for further study/intervention.

Racial and ethnic classification in these applied settings share a common feature: the population groupings recognized are often problem-specific (Crews and Bindon 1991; Molnar 1983). They do not necessarily reflect evolutionary histories and, in fact, may serve as proxies for both genetic and environmental influences on the variables of interest (Buehler et al. 1989; Damon 1971). However, while applied bioanthropologists may approach racial and ethnic classification from a somewhat special perspective, they share a global concern with other researchers: reliability of the data once a classification system has been defined.

A variety of factors are known to influence the reliability of racial identifications. Self-reported racial data are generally acknowledged to be more accurate than those estimated by an observer (Brues 1977). However, when self-reported racial and ethnic data are obtained from questionnaires, the terminology used, the form of the question, and even their proximity to other questions can influence subject responses (Farley 1990). In addition, Census Bureau research indicates that ethnic minority groups such as Negroes, Mexicans, and Puerto Ricans provide more consistent responses than do subjects with Western European origins, and that reliability of ethnicity data in American whites is inversely related to the number of generations one's family has been in the United States (Johnson 1974).

Racial and ethnic data reliability are of particular concern in such widely-used reference data bases as those maintained by the Census Bureau and by the Department of Defense. In this article, we specifically contrast racial and ethnic questionnaire data in an official U.S. Army data base with identifications made by interview with an anthropologist. The racial/ethnic classification model used is that of Federal Directive 15 (1978): white, not of Hispanic Origin; black, not of Hispanic Origin; Hispanic; Asian or Pacific Islander; American Indian or Alaskan Native.

## Materials and Methods

Subjects in this study were drawn from 23,560 active-duty enlisted soldiers screened during sample selection for the 1988 U.S. Army Anthropometric Survey (ANSUR) (Gordon et al. 1989). Random samples of 100 males and 100 females each were drawn from five racial groupings: whites, blacks, Hispanics, Asian/Pacific Islanders, and mixed-race individuals. Sample sizes were smaller for American Indians, where a 100 percent sample rendered only 92 males and 54 females. Table 1 presents a race-specific summary of the most frequently declared ethnicities in these study groups.

Individuals were matched by gender, birth date, and name to their official 1988 U.S. Army records derived from DD Form 1966/1 and maintained by the Personnel Information Systems Command (PERSINSCOM). Because racial classification in the PERSINSCOM system differs slightly from the ANSUR system, some recoding was required before racial identifications in the two systems could be fairly compared.

Table 2 illustrates racial and ethnic classification in the two systems. Both comply with Federal Directive 15 (Federal Register 1978) in that a separate Hispanic group is either directly or indirectly identifiable in addition to four traditional racial groups: whites, blacks, Asian/Pacific Islanders, and American Indians/Alaskan Natives. The PERSINSCOM racial classification, however, does not directly identify Hispanics. Instead, cross-classification with the PERSINSCOM ethnicity categories Cuban, Latin American of Hispanic Descent, Mexican, Puerto Rican, and other Hispanic creates the necessary Hispanic category. Similarly, PERSINSCOM does not identify Pacific Islanders in its racial classification system, so cross-classification with ethnicity codes Micronesian, Melanesian, and other Pacific Islander is used to meet the Federal Directive 15 requirement.

A crucial feature of the PERSINSCOM system is the absence of a category for individuals of mixed racial heritage and the fact that no instructions are provided regarding the disposition of such people in primary categories. In contrast, ANSUR racial classification required that parentage be 75 percent or higher in the nonmixed categories (similar to Hazuda et al. 1986), and data on parental race, ethnicity, and birthplace were used to verify each subject's classification. ANSUR subjects of mixed-race were

**Table 1**
**Ethnic Frequencies in the Study Sample**

| Race | Ethnicity | |
|---|---|---|
| White (*n* = 200) | American | 69.00% |
| | German | 12.50% |
| | Irish | 5.00% |
| | English | 2.50% |
| | Italian | 2.50% |
| | | 91.50% |
| Black (*n* = 200) | Black/Negro/Afro-American | 79.00% |
| | American | 18.00% |
| | | 97.00% |
| Hispanic (*n* = 200) | Puerto Rican | 41.00% |
| | Mexican | 14.50% |
| | Mexican American | 15.00% |
| | Hispanic American | 10.00% |
| | American | 5.00% |
| | Dominican | 3.50% |
| | | 89.00% |
| Asian/Pacific Islander (*n* = 200) | Filipino | 40.00% |
| | Samoan | 15.50% |
| | Chamorro | 11.50% |
| | Korean | 9.00% |
| | Japanese | 6.00% |
| | Hawaiian | 3.00% |
| | | 85.00% |
| Amerindian (*n* = 146) | Navajo | 18.50% |
| | Cherokee | 13.70% |
| | Sioux | 11.60% |
| | Native American/American Indian | 6.90% |
| | Lumbee | 5.50% |
| | Chippewa | 4.80% |
| | | 61.00% |
| Mixed (*n* = 200) | American | 45.50% |
| | Black/Negro-American | 18.00% |
| | Puerto Rican | 9.80% |
| | Filipino | 9.40% |
| | Mexican American | 4.20% |
| | Hispanic American | 4.00% |
| | | 90.90% |

classified separately and encouraged to specify two or more racial components as further identifiers. In this study, the disposition of mixed-race indi-

**Table 2**
**PERSINSCOM and ANSUR Race and Ethnicity Categories**

| PERSINSCOM Race | ANSUR Race |
|---|---|
| White | White, not of Hispanic Origin |
| Black | Black, not of Hispanic Origin |
| | Hispanic |
| Asian | Asian/Pacific Islander |
| American Indian/Alaskan Native | American Indian/Alaskan Native |
| Other (Specify) | Other (Specify) |
| Unknown | Unknown |
| | Mixed (Specify) |

| PERSINSCOM Ethnicity | ANSUR Ethnicity |
|---|---|
| None | Fill in the Blank |
| Other | |
| Cuban | |
| Latin American (Hispanic) | |
| Mexican | |
| Puerto Rican | |
| Other Hispanic | |
| Chinese | |
| Filipino | |
| Japanese | |
| Korean | |
| Vietnamese | |
| Indian | |
| Other Asian | |
| Micronesian | |
| Melanesian | |
| Other Pacific Islander | |
| Aleut | |
| Eskimo | |
| U.S./Canadian Tribes | |
| Other American Indian | |
| Unknown | |

viduals within the PERSINSCOM system is addressed descriptively as a separate problem altogether.

It should be noted that methods of administration differ significantly between ANSUR and PERSINSCOM data bases. Directions for the administration of DD Form 1966/1 indicate that "the applicant, under supervision of recruiter" completes both the race and ethnicity elements of the form (Army Regulation 601-210, U.S. Army 1990). The form itself does not define race or ethnicity, nor does it list acceptable choices for ethnicity. This information is presumably provided by the recruiter, who has access to an Army Regulation (AR 601-210) in which more detailed direction is given.

ANSUR race and birthplace questions were also administered by questionnaire; however, these data were checked for consistency by an anthropologist during an interview to determine each subject's ethnicity. Ethnicity interviews involved using synonyms to explain the concept, including national origin, family heritage, family descent, family ancestry, and cultural affiliation or family tradition. Examples were occasionally provided, but in no cases were appropriate responses suggested or supplied for the respondent.

Because the ANSUR data included supporting information on parental race, ethnicity, and birthplace, and because they involved interview, review, and reconciliation of inconsistencies on site in the presence of the subject, ANSUR determinations of race and ethnicity are treated in this study as the reference data against which PERSINSCOM records are compared.

## Results

Table 3 presents rates of concordant racial classification in the 1,146 soldiers studied. Overall, only 687 of 946 subjects (73 percent) in the five primary racial classes had concordant racial/ethnic codes present in the PERSINSCOM data base. Racial misclassification is not evenly distributed across groups; no misclassification occurs in whites and blacks, whereas misclassification rates for army minority groups are 43 percent for American Indians, 48 percent for Hispanics, and 50 percent for Asian/Pacific Islanders.

### *Misclassification of Hispanic Soldiers*

Table 4 presents an overview of Hispanic classifications in the PERSINSCOM data base. Upon review, only one of the 96 Hispanic misclassifications in Table 4 can be attributed to a "mistake." In that case, the

**Table 3**
**Racial Misclassification Results**

| Subject's Race | PERSINSCOM Code(s) | # Correct |
|---|---|---|
| White | White | 200/200 (100%) |
| Black | Black | 200/200 (100%) |
| Hispanic | White or Black or Other w/Hispanic Ethnicity | 104/200 (52%) |
| Asian/PI | Asian or Other w/PI Ethnicity | 100/200 (50%) |
| American Indian | American Indian | 93/146 (57%) |

**Table 4**
**Classification of Hispanic Soldiers in PERSINSCOM**

| PERSINSCOM Ethnic Group | PERSINSCOM Race | | | | | |
|---|---|---|---|---|---|---|
| | White | Black | Asian | American Indian | Other | Total |
| Hispanic[a] | 22 | 2 | 0 | 0 | 80 | 104 |
| Non-Hispanic | 0 | 0 | 0 | 0 | 1 | 1 |
| Other | 55 | 6 | 0 | 0 | 34 | 95 |
| Totals | 77 | 8 | 0 | 0 | 115 | 200 |

[a]Hispanic ethnicity codes in PERSINSCOM are: Cuban, Latin American of Hispanic Descent, Mexican, Puerto Rican, and Other Hispanic.

subject was incorrectly identified as being a U.S./Canadian Indian when neither he nor his parents are Indian. The other 95 Hispanic misclassification had either a blank ($n$ = 1) or "Other" ($n$ = 94) PERSINSCOM ethnicity code, and therefore could not be identified as Hispanic in the PERSINSCOM system. Such frequent use of category "Other" by Hispanics is unexpected, because "Other Hispanic" is also a PERSINSCOM ethnicity category.

Chi-Square testing of the five most frequent Hispanic ethnic groups (see Table 5) indicated that actual ethnic affiliation is not significantly associated with PERSINSCOM ethnic category "Other" (chi-square = 1.58, $df$ = 4, $p$ = .813). So at least in the five most frequent ethnicities, all Hispanics are equally likely to be misclassified in this way.

Because Hispanic identification in the PERSINSCOM system requires specific ethnicity data, extensive use of nonspecific ethnicity codes such as "Other" can contribute to underestimation of Hispanic representation in

**Table 5**
**Hispanic Misclassifications Reported by ANSUR Ethnicity[a]**

| Ethnic Group | Racial Classification | | Totals |
|---|---|---|---|
| | Correct | Incorrect | |
| American | 5 | 5 | 10 |
| Hispanic American | 8 | 11 | 19 |
| Mexican | 28 | 31 | 59 |
| Puerto Rican | 52 | 29 | 81 |
| Totals | 93 | 76 | 169 |

[a]Only the four most frequently named ethnic groups are reported.
[b]Chi-Square = 5.50, $df$ = 3, $p$ = .138.

the army. In this study, nonspecific ethnicity data are almost exclusively responsible for a 48 percent (96/200) underestimation of Hispanics in the PERSINSCOM data base.

Although the magnitude of Hispanic underestimation in this study is disconcerting, it is not unique. Verdugo and Grafton (1988) note that Hispanic recruit frequencies based upon the 1986 New Recruit Survey were 7.6 percent, whereas an estimate based on official army data for these same subjects would have yielded a 3.4 percent figure. This amounts to an underestimation of approximately 55 percent in recruits, which is very close to our own figure of 48 percent in permanent party soldiers. Verdugo and Grafton (1988) attribute underestimation of Hispanic recruits to the fact that recruiters are filling out DD 1966/1 and may be reluctant to ask what they consider to be socially sensitive questions. In addition, race and ethnicity questions on the New Recruit Survey included a specific yes/no Hispanic ancestry question that may render a more accurate estimate of Hispanic representation than reliance upon declaration of a specific Hispanic ethnic group such as Mexican, Cuban, Puerto Rican.

### *Misclassification of American Indian Soldiers*

As can be seen in Table 6, discordant racial classification occurred in 63 of 146 American Indian/Alaskan Native subjects (43 percent). Of those misclassified, 36 were identified as white, one as Asian, one as black, and 25 as other.

Chi-Square testing of soldiers with four American Indian grandparents (as determined by selfreported parental race) versus those with three of four Indian grandparents (see Table 7) indicates that there is a significant association between degree of Indian parentage and identification as Indian within PERSINSCOM (chi-square = 6.31, $df = 1$, $p = .012$). In this study, American Indians are 2.9 times more likely to be correctly classified within the PERSINSCOM system if both parents are also classified as American Indian.

Only 14 of the 63 misclassified American Indians had legitimate PERSINSCOM American Indian ethnic codes, so cross-classification with PERSINSCOM ethnicity could not substantially reduce American Indian racial underestimation in that system, even if it were added as an adjunct to the explicit American Indian/Alaskan Native racial code. Furthermore, only 40 of the 83 American Indians *correctly* classified by PERSINSCOM had legitimate Indian ethnicities in the PERSINSCOM system. Clearly PERSINSCOM ethnicity codes for U.S./Canadian Tribes, Eskimos, and Aleuts are not being used for the vast majority of Native American soldiers in this study. In fact, ethnicity was coded as "Other" for 84 of 146 American Indian soldiers, despite the fact that all but 12 of these 84 cited specific tribal affiliations during ANSUR interviews, and 10 of the remaining 12 chose "Native American," "American Indian," or some variant thereof.

**Table 6**
**Classification of American Indian Soldiers in PERSINSCOM**

| | PERSINSCOM Race | | | | | |
|---|---|---|---|---|---|---|
| PERSINSCOM Ethnic Group | White | Black | Asian | American Indian | Other | Total |
| Indian[a] | 2 | 0 | 1 | 40 | 11 | 54 |
| Non-Indian | 0 | 0 | 0 | 4 | 4 | 8 |
| Other | 34 | 1 | 0 | 39 | 10 | 84 |
| Totals | 36 | 1 | 1 | 83 | 25 | 146 |

[a]American Indian ethnicity codes in PERSINSCOM are: U.S./Canadian Tribes, Eskimo, and Aleut.

**Table 7**
**American Indian Misclassification by Parentage**

| | Racial Classification | | |
|---|---|---|---|
| Indian Parentage | Correct | Incorrect | Totals |
| 3 Grandparents | 10 | 18 | 28 |
| 4 Grandparents | 73 | 45 | 118 |
| Totals | 83 | 63 | 146 |

[a]Chi-Square = 6.31, $df = 1$, $p = .012$.

Chi-Square testing of the four most frequent American Indian ethnicities indicates that tribal affiliation is significantly associated with racial misclassification (see Table 8). Navajo soldiers are 6.6 times more likely to be correctly classified by race than are Cherokee soldiers. Sioux soldiers are 4.3 times more likely to be correctly classified by race than are Cherokee soldiers.

As can be seen from the data above, misclassification of American Indians in the PERSINSCOM system is a serious problem. Based upon this study, which included *only* Indian soldiers with three of four grandparents also Indian, 43 percent of American Indians may not be identified as such in their official records. The fact that soldiers with four Indian grandparents are more likely to be correctly identified than those with three suggests that degree of admixture may be related to probability of misclassification. The fact that Navajo and Sioux soldiers are more likely to be correctly identified than Cherokee would also be consistent with this hypothesis (Spicer 1980; Stein et al. 1965; Williams et al. 1985).

One explanation for high American Indian misclassification rates is that recruiters are relying on visual inspection and using category "Other"

**Table 8**
**American Indian Misclassifications Reported by ANSUR Ethnicity***

| | Racial Classification | | |
|---|---|---|---|
| Ethnic Group | Correct | Incorrect | Totals |
| Cherokee | 6 | 14 | 20 |
| Native American | 5 | 5 | 10 |
| Navajo | 20 | 7 | 27 |
| Sioux | 11 | 6 | 17 |
| Totals | 42 | 32 | 74 |

[a]Only the four most frequently named ethnic groups are reported.
[b]Chi-Square = 9.76, $df = 3$, $p = .021$.

when they are not certain. Individuals with less admixture may look more "Indian" and are therefore more likely to be correctly classified. Significantly higher rates of American Indian identification were also obtained in the 1970 census when self-report rather than interviewer observation was used (Brues 1977).

*Misclassification of Asian and Pacific Island Soldiers*

Asians and Pacific Islanders also had high rates of discordance with PERSINSCOM codes: misclassification occurred in 100 of 200 cases (see Table 9).

A chi-square test (see Table 10) of Asian versus Pacific Island subjects indicates that there is no significant difference in misclassification rates in these groups. Of the Asian misclassifications, nine were coded white, one was coded black, one was coded American Indian, and 53 were coded as "Other." Large numbers of "Other" race codes in Asian soldiers are puzzling because 36 of the 53 (68 percent) had legitimate Asian ethnicities in the PERSINSCOM data base, and all declared Asian ethnic affiliations during ANSUR interviews. Of the Pacific Islander misclassifications, five were coded white, and 31 were coded as "Other" with either nonspecific (24/31) or non-Pacific Islander (7/31) ethnic codes in the PERSINSCOM data base. In contrast, some 35 of the 36 declared Pacific Island ethnicities during ANSUR interviews.

Table 11 presents a cross-tabulation of misclassification for the four most frequent Asian and Pacific Islander ethnic groups. Misclassification rates are similar for Filipinos and Samoans: 45 and 43 percent respectively. Chamorro soldiers, however, are 1.2 times more likely to be misclassified than Samoans, and Koreans are 4.6 times less likely to be misclassified than are Filipinos. It is likely that the "visual identification" hypothesis pre-

**Table 9**
**Classification of Asian and Pacific Islander Soldiers**

| PERSINSCOM Ethnic Group | PERSINSCOM Race: White | Black | Asian | American Indian | Other | Totals |
|---|---|---|---|---|---|---|
| Asian | 1 | 0 | 38 | 0 | 42 | 81 |
| Pacific Islander | 1 | 0 | 1 | 0 | 30 | 32 |
| Non A/PI | 0 | 0 | 0 | 0 | 1 | 1 |
| Other | 12 | 1 | 31 | 1 | 41 | 86 |
| Totals | 14 | 1 | 70 | 1 | 114 | 200 |

**Table 10**
**Classification Accuracy of Asians and Pacific Islanders**

| Ethnic Group | Racial Classification: Correct | Incorrect | Totals |
|---|---|---|---|
| Asians | 66 | 64 | 130 |
| Pacific Islanders | 34 | 36 | 70 |
| Totals | 100 | 100 | 200 |

[a]Chi-Square = .088, *df* = 1, *p* = .767.

**Table 11**
**Asian/Pacific Islander Misclassifications by ANSUR Ethnicity[a]**

| Ethnic Group | Racial Classification: Correct | Incorrect | Totals |
|---|---|---|---|
| Filipino | 36 | 44 | 80 |
| Korean | 15 | 4 | 19 |
| Chamorro | 9 | 14 | 23 |
| Samoan | 14 | 18 | 32 |
| Totals | 74 | 80 | 154 |

[a]Only the four most frequently named ethnic groups are reported.
[b]Chi-Square = 8.53, *df* = 3, *p* = .036.

**Table 12**
**Racial Distribution of Mixed-Race Soldiers**

| Secondary Race | Primary Race | | | | | |
|---|---|---|---|---|---|---|
| | White | Black | Hispanic | Asian | American Indian | Totals |
| White | 0 | 26 | 21 | 13 | 23 | 83 |
| Black | 6 | 0 | 8 | 2 | 5 | 21 |
| Hispanic | 22 | 10 | 0 | 3 | 1 | 36 |
| Asian | 16 | 7 | 1 | 0 | 0 | 24 |
| American Indian | 11 | 21 | 3 | 1 | 0 | 36 |
| Totals | 55 | 64 | 33 | 19 | 29 | 200 |

viously advanced for American Indian misclassifications may also be appropriate here.

*Soldiers of Mixed Racial Ancestry*

The disposition of mixed-race soldiers within official classification systems is not merely a matter of curiosity: the prevalence of mixed-race soldiers based on the ANSUR data base is estimated at 4.4 percent of the army. Table 12 presents a cross-tabulation of the primary and secondary racial groups for 200 randomly selected mixed-race soldiers. Primary racial group is defined as that category mentioned first by the subject.

As can be seen in Table 13, the rate of concordance between PERSINSCOM race and the subjects' self-reported primary race varied significantly among racial groups (chi-square = 81.127, $df = 4$, $p < .001$). In particular, concordant racial codes in "primarily" black subjects were five times more likely than for "primarily" white subjects; 26 times more likely than for "primarily" Asian/Pacific Islanders; 43 times more likely than "primarily" American Indians; and 70 times more likely than for "primarily" Hispanics. These results closely parallel previous observations that racial misclassification is greatest in the army's minorities: Hispanics, Asian/Pacific Islanders, and American Indians.

PERSINSCOM racial codes corresponded with the subjects' self-reported *secondary* race in 69 of 200 subjects. Overall then, the PERSINSCOM racial classification of these subjects corresponded to either their primary or secondary race 84 percent of the time. While this might seem unusually high given the discordant classifications in other portions of the PERSINSCOM data base, it should be noted that racial classification concordance was 100 percent in whites and blacks, and more than half the primary racial codes in this mixed-race study group are either white or black.

**Table 13**
**Correspondence between PERSINSCOM Race and Self-Reported Primary Race in Soldiers of Mixed Racial Ancestry**

| PERSINSCOM Race | Primary Race | | | | | Totals |
|---|---|---|---|---|---|---|
| | White | Black | Hispanic | Asian | American Indian | |
| Concordant | 32 | 56 | 3 | 4 | 4 | 99 |
| Discordant | 23 | 8 | 30 | 15 | 25 | 101 |
| Totals | 55 | 64 | 33 | 19 | 29 | 200 |

[a]Chi-Square = 81.13, $df = 4$, $p < .001$.

## Discussion

The levels of Hispanic, Asian, and American Indian misclassification observed in this study have serious consequences in an applied setting. The army's official anthropometric data bases, for example, are race matched to PERSINSCOM distributions to ensure that materiel systems are designed on data that are representative of the contemporary army population. Significant underrepresentation of minority groups that have unique body size and shape distributions will result in protective clothing ensembles that systematically fit minorities poorly.

The levels of Asian and American Indian misclassification observed, the failure to identify individuals of mixed race, and the generally poor quality ethnicity data all will hamper forensic identifications of army casualties that rely on official records. Reliance on family-provided history should help to solve this problem.

It is ironic that minority groups most likely to report their ethnicity consistently according to the Census Bureau (Johnson 1974) are least likely to have correct racial/ethnic classifications in official army records. Several features of the PERSINSCOM system may be contributing to this result. Firstly, although racial/ethnic data are supposed to be self-reported, anecdotal information (Anonymous 1991; Verdugo and Grafton 1988) suggests that army recruiters are filling out the forms themselves, perhaps with little input from the recruit. In addition, the forms themselves lack adequate definitions of the terms "race" and "ethnicity" and their categories. Secondly, racial and ethnic categories "Other," which are of little use in classification, are used extensively even though individuals are clearly capable of providing more specific answers. Thirdly, reliance on ethnic cross-classification to recast PERSINSCOM data into the groupings required by Federal Directive 15 requires a level of ethnic specificity and reliance not currently present in this system.

Several specific recommendations are offered. Firstly, when identification of Hispanic individuals is required, as it is in many anthropological projects, either there should be a separate Hispanic category provided under the race question, or there should be a separate question altogether that requires a yes-or-no answer regarding Hispanic ancestry. Secondly, there should be either an open-ended ethnicity question or a more extensive list of ethnicities, such as that used in the 1980 Census (Farley 1990). This would decrease abuse of the "Other" categories. Finally, the system should not rely on a separately published army regulation to provide terminology guidance. This should be printed on the form or on its back, and the recruit should always be the one to answer these questions.

## References Cited

Anonymous
1991 Telephone Conversation between Nancy Bell, Geocenters, Inc., and a U.S. Army Recruiting Sergeant who asked to remain anonymous.
Brues, A. M.
1977 People and Races. New York: Macmillan.
Buehler, J. W., D. F. Stroup, D. N. Klaucke, and R. L. Berkelman
1989 The Reporting of Race and Ethnicity in the National Notifiable Diseases Surveillance System. Public Health Reports 104(5):457–465.
Crews, D. E., and J. R. Bindon
1991 Ethnicity as a Taxonomic Tool in Biomedical and Biosocial Research. Ethnicity and Disease 1(Winter):42–49.
Damon, A.
1971 Race, Ethnic Group, and Disease. *In* The Biological and Social Meaning of Race. R. H. Osborne, ed. Pp. 57–74. San Francisco, CA: W. H. Freeman.
Farley, R.
1990 Race, Ancestry and Spanish Origin: Findings from the 1980's and Questions for the 1990's. Paper presented at the 150th Annual Meeting of the American Statistical Association, Anaheim, California, August 6–9.
Federal Register
1978 Race and Ethnic Standards for Federal Statistics and Administrative Reporting. Directive No. 15 Federal Register 43(87):19269.
Gordon, C. C., T. Churchill, C. E. Clauser, B. Bradtmiller, J. T. McConville, I. Tebbetts, and R. A. Walker
1989 1988 Anthropometric Survey of U.S. Army Personnel: Methods and Summary Statistics. Technical Report 89/044. Natick, MA: U.S. Army Natick Research, Development, and Engineering Center.
Hazuda, H. P., P. J. Comeaux, M. P. Stern, S. M. Haffner, C. W. Eifler, and M. Rosenthal
1986 A Comparison of Three Indicators for Identifying Mexican Americans in Epidemiologic Research: Methodological Findings from the San Antonio Heart Study. American Journal of Epidemiology 123(1):96–111.
Johnson, C. E.
1974 Consistency of Reporting of Ethnic Origin in the Current Population Survey. Bureau of the Census Technical Paper 31. Washington, DC: U.S. Department of Commerce.
Molnar, S.
1983 Human Variation. Englewood Cliffs, NJ: Prentice-Hall.
Spicer, E. H.
1980 American Indians. *In* Harvard Encyclopedia of American Ethnic Groups. S. Thernstrom, ed. Pp. 58–114. Cambridge: Belknap Press.
Stein, J. H., K. M. West, J. M. Robey, D. F. Tirador, and G. W. McDonald
1965 The High Prevalence of Abnormal Glucose Tolerance in the Cherokee Indians of North Carolina. Archives of Internal Medicine 116:842–845.
U.S. Army
1990 Regular Army and Army Reserve Enlistment Program. Department of the Army. Army Regulation 601–210.

Verdugo, N. V., and F. C. Grafton
1988 An Overview of Hispanics in the Active Enlisted Army: 1980–1986. Technical Report 802. Manpower and Personnel Research Laboratory, U.S. Army Research Institute for the Behavioral and Social Sciences, Alexandria, VA.

Williams, R. C., A. G. Steinberg, P. Gershowitz, P. H. Bennett, W. C. Knowler, D. J. Pettitt, W. Butler, R. Baird, L. Dowda-Rea, T. A. Burch, H. G. Morse, and C. G. Smith
1985 GM Allotypes in Native Americans: Evidence for Three Distinct Migrations across the Bering Land Bridge. American Journal of Physical Anthropology 66:1–19.

# Race, Ethnicity, and Forensic Anthropology

## Realities of Racial Determination in a Forensic Setting

Madeleine J. Hinkes

The role of a forensic anthropologist is to assist the medical examiner in the process of death investigation, usually by helping to identify the remains. To do this, the anthropologist makes the necessary observations and measurements to determine sex, age, race, stature, and any unique biological features (such as healed fractures). The most difficult assessment is often race, which may seem surprising because we so automatically register the race of people with whom we come in contact. The fact is, when we remove the most obvious racial cues, such as skin color, hair morphology, and eye shape, the remaining evidence can be ambiguous. Even though we have only three major categories from which to choose, the choice is not easy for a variety of reasons: individuals who may be classified in the same race can vary greatly in physical appearance; the tremendous variation in physical appearance is reflected in a similar variation in skeletal remains, even though skeletal features may not correlate with particular features of soft tissue anatomy; there are few if any population-specific markers; the amount of racial admixture increases almost daily. Nevertheless, an assessment of racial affinity must be made with some degree of certainty, if the biological remains are to be placed in their antemortem social context.

### Anthropological Race

The concept of race has long been a topic of discussion and debate in the field of physical anthropology, because it is so closely related to the central tenets of variation, adaptability, and evolution. Following in the Linnean flurry to classify was J. F. Blumenbach (1752–1840), the "Father of Physical Anthropology," who delineated five major races: Caucasoid, Mongoloid, American Indian, Ethiopian, and Malay (Brace and Montagu 1965). Current-day anthropologists recognize at least three major races, namely, Caucasoid, Mongoloid, and Negroid, which differ from each other with respect to skin color, facial structure, hair form, body proportions, and morbidity and mortality patterns. These major subdivisions are in common usage because they are the easiest to distinguish and the categories most often used by nonscientists. An Australoid racial group is also recognized.

The Mongoloid group is frequently divided into Mongoloid (Oriental), American Indian, and Polynesian (Gill 1986).

The racial classification of choice is influenced by one's preferred definition of race. The population genetics definition is a breeding population, a group of people sharing a set of common features that differ systematically from other such sets in correspondence with geographic areas (Brues 1977; Garn 1971; Gill 1990; Molnar 1975). Commonalities derive from a common (albeit remote) ancestor and are the result of ordering genetic variability in response to selective forces present in the environment. In nonhuman species, continuing geographic isolation stimulates speciation. In the human species, such events as wars, colonization, and migration have served to break down the isolation and the accompanying physical and genetic distinctions among populations. Yet the world will never be homogeneous, and we as anthropologists can take great pleasure in the visible evidence of human diversity.

Every individual has a racial identity; however, one's social race or "ethnicity" may not be the same as his biological race. For example, self-proclaimed "Hispanic" individuals may be Spanish (Caucasoid), Mexican (American Indian), Puerto Rican (Negroid admixture), or Filipino (Asian Mongoloid). Someone with one-eighth American Indian blood may in some jurisdictions legally classify himself as American Indian, even if he is a blue-eyed blond. We cannot know where a deceased individual placed himself on the racial continuum, but we can determine from his remains the preponderance of the various characteristics more often associated with one race over another. It can be a fascinating and frustrating exercise to attempt to read one's racial history in a person's remains.

## Racial Traits

Those physical features we have come to rely on as racial traits differ in frequency of occurrence or degree of development among races. There are no archetypes, no typological listings of tried-and-true rules. As no trait is entirely racial, so also is no trait entirely without some racial meaning. For a trait to be racially diagnostic, there must be a geographic component: high frequency in one part of the world, low in others (Brues 1990). As in the rest of the natural world, boundaries are arbitrary; racial differences are clinal rather than discrete.

Rarely is it a simple case of trait presence/absence; nearly all traits show gradations or degrees of development. The paradox here is that for a trait to be a useful racial marker—be it a visual observation or a metric calculation—it must truly discriminate between populations, and there must be a reliable way of comparing a forensic specimen to some norm (Brues 1990). There are dozens of cranial, facial, dental, and postcranial features that fit this need to various extents (Krogman and Iscan 1986; Stewart 1979).

**Table 1**
**Craniofacial Trait Variations Common to Each Geographical Race**

| | Mongoloid | American Indian | Caucasoid | Polynesian | Negroid |
|---|---|---|---|---|---|
| Cranial Form | Broad | Medium-Broad | Medium | Highly Variable | Long |
| Sagittal Outline | High, Globular | Medium-Low; Sloping Frontal | High, Rounded | Medium | Highly Variable; Post-Bregmatic Depression |
| Nose Form | Medium | Medium | Narrow | Medium | Broad |
| Nasal Bone Size | Small | Medium/ Large | Large | Medium | Medium/ Small |
| Nasal Profile | Concave | Concavo-Convex | Straight | Concave/ Concavo-Convex | Straight/ Concave |
| Nasal Spine | Medium | Medium, Tilted | Prominent Straight | Highly Variable | Reduced |
| Nasal Sill | Medium | Medium | Sharp | Dull/ Absent | Dull/ Absent |
| Incisor Form | Shovelled | Shovelled | Blade | Blade | Blade |
| Facial Prognathism | Moderate | Moderate | Reduced | Moderate | Extreme |
| Alveolar Prognathism | Moderate | Moderate | Reduced | Moderate | Extreme |
| Malar Form | Projecting | Projecting | Reduced | Projecting | Reduced |
| Palatal Form | Parabolic Elliptic | Elliptic | Parabolic | Parabolic/ Elliptic | Hyperbolic |
| Orbital Form | Round | Rhomboid | Rhomboid | Rhomboid | Round |
| Mandible | Robust | Robust | Medium | Robust; Rocker Form | Gracile; Oblique Gonial Angle |
| Chin Projection | Moderate | Moderate | Prominent | Moderate | Reduced |
| Chin Form | Median | Median | Bilateral | Median | Median |

*Source*: Gill 1986:149.

Table 1 (Gill 1986:149) is included here because it supports Gill's contention that differences in skeletal features of the face alone are sufficient to allow separation of over 75 percent of the members of one of the five racial groups from members of all others (Gill 1990:viii). Brues (1977, 1990) takes this even further by concentrating mainly on the nasal root area.

Note that these are all morphological traits, most of which are not amenable to exact measurement. There are also useful metric indices for this region of the body (Giles and Elliot 1962; Gill 1986; Howells 1970). Judgments based on metric rather than morphological observations project an air of greater precision, even though this may not be a realistic depiction of the hazy boundaries between races. Hooton stated early on that "morphological features which can be observed and described but cannot be measured are probably of greater anthropological significance than diameters and indices" (Brues 1990:2). It is important not to be ruled by numbers but to keep in mind what is being measured and how it is meaningful. This point becomes significant in forensic applications, because skeletal series used in the lab to devise some of these measures often do not reflect what we actually see in forensic cases.

## The Forensic Setting

In the forensic setting, the problem is not so much one of classification as it is of identification. The medical examiner does not want a theoretical discussion of race, he wants one word to fill in the blank space on a form. It is up to the anthropologist to categorize the unknown remains in terms that reflect racial reality as understood in that particular region (Stewart 1979). If the remains show evidence of admixture, that should be noted. It used to be that most remains were Negroid or Caucasoid, with American Indian seen in some parts of the country. Now we are seeing a significant Asian component and finding that what worked to define American Indians falls short of defining Asians. Much more research is needed (Brooks et al. 1990).

In the context of admixture, I subscribe to Stewart's philosophy that sometimes it is only the anthropologist's experience that tells him there is an undefinable "something" about the skeleton that suggests one race over another (1979:231). However, when testifying in court, a more convincing statement is usually required. This is where metrics can be used to support a visual observation. Even those morphological structures that are not easily measured, such as the nasal root area, still need to be quantified in terms of their frequency among various populations (Brues 1990).

The nature of the remains affects the ease of racial determination. We see bodies that are intact, decomposed, burned, cremated, mutilated, skeletal, and fragmentary. Therefore it is mandatory that the anthropologist be familiar with racial traits throughout the body, in case preferred areas are not present. If identification hinges on the findings of the anthropologist, he or she may not have the luxury of days or weeks to run every conceivable laboratory analysis. Accurate, reliable decisions need to be made expeditiously.

The incompleteness of body parts may preclude the taking of specific measurements necessary for discriminant functions. This is one reason why my own bias has been toward qualitative observations rather than quantitative. Even if only a portion of the particular structure is present, the observer can still get a feel for its racial affinity. Flesh-covered remains may be difficult to measure without considerable dissection, but then so many other visual clues are present in fleshed remains. It is important to realize that not all remains seen will be skeletal; the classic descriptions of body proportions and hair form and distribution will come in handy, as will remembering to look in protected body areas (e.g., underarms) for skin color in burned remains.

I have found facial and dental traits to be most useful. Even in a body traumatized in an aircraft mishap, there are usually enough remnants of chin, malar, nasal root, or nasal sill by which to assess race. Failing that, the remaining teeth should hold some clues. But in a recent case—the skeletal remains of a Vietnam War air crash victim—there was virtually no cranial or dental material. The only evidence for race was a remarkably long and straight femur, the only unbroken bone among the remains. This feature strongly suggested Negroid ancestry (Stewart 1962), which was supported by use of DiBennardo and Taylor's (1983) discriminant function based on measurements of the femur and hip bone. The remains fell well within the black range; on the basis of race and age they could then be associated with the one unaccounted for member of an aircrew.

Subadults are more difficult to assess, but a number of diagnostic dental features are apparent in the deciduous dentition (Hinkes 1986), and facial prognathism is developed at a young age.

A skilled eye and practiced judgment are the most valuable tools for a forensic anthropologist. Increasing experience will allow him to make sense out of small bits of evidence. We are applying anthropological techniques to very real problems of identification and continually testing ourselves. Any errors we make may result in remains not being identified. We must adopt a flexible attitude toward racial designations and, if we are proven wrong, turn an evaluation of error into a contribution that will facilitate improved estimates in the future (Rathbun and Buikstra 1984:224). We need to observe the variation in living people around us and continue to document that variation in known series, recognizing the effects of immigration and admixture. After all, adaptation is the recurring theme of physical anthropology; we are seeing evolution in action.

## References Cited

Brace, C. L., and A. Montagu
1965 Man's Evolution. New York: Macmillan.

Brooks, S., R. H. Brooks, and D. France
1990 Alveolar Prognathism Contour, An Aspect of Racial Identification. *In* Skeletal Attribution of Race. G. W. Gill and S. Rhine, eds. Pp. 41–46. Albuquerque, NM: Maxwell Museum of Anthropology, Anthropological Papers No. 4.
Brues, A. M.
1977 People and Races. New York: Macmillan.
1990 The Once and Future Diagnosis of Race. *In* Skeletal Attribution of Race. G. W. Gill and S. Rhine, eds. Pp. 1–8. Albuquerque, NM: Maxwell Museum of Anthropology, Anthropological Papers No. 4.
DiBennardo, R., and J. V. Taylor
1983 Multiple Discriminant Function Analysis of Sex and Race in the Postcranial Skeleton. American Journal of Physical Anthropology 61:305–314.
Garn, S. M.
1971 Human Races. Springfield, IL: Charles C Thomas.
Giles, E., and O. Elliot
1962 Race Identification from Cranial Measurements. Journal of Forensic Sciences 7:147–157.
Gill, G. W.
1986 Craniofacial Criteria in Forensic Race Identification. *In* Forensic Osteology. K. J. Reichs, ed. Pp. 143–159. Springfield, IL: Charles C Thomas.
1990 Introduction. *In* Skeletal Attribution of Race. G. W. Gill and S. Rhine, eds. Pp. vii–xii. Albuquerque, NM: Maxwell Museum of Anthropology, Anthropological Papers No. 4.
Hinkes, M. J.
1986 Racial Characteristics of the Deciduous Dentition. Paper presented to the American Academy of Forensic Sciences, Cincinnati.
Howells, W. W.
1970 Multivariate Analysis for the Identification of Race from the Crania. *In* Personal Identification in Mass Disasters. T. D. Stewart, ed. Pp. 111–123. Washington, DC: American Museum of Natural History.
Krogman, W. M., and M. Y. Iscan
1986 The Human Skeleton in Forensic Medicine. Springfield, IL: Charles C Thomas.
Molnar, S.
1975 Races, Types, and Ethnic Groups. Englewood Cliffs, NJ: Prentice-Hall.
Rathbun, T. A., and J. E. Buikstra, eds.
1984 Human Identification. Springfield, IL: Charles C Thomas.
Stewart, T. D.
1962 Anterior Femoral Curvature: Its Utility for Race Identification. Human Biology 34:49–62.
1979 Essentials of Forensic Anthropology. Springfield, IL: Charles C Thomas.

# Skeletal Criteria for Racial Attribution

Stanley Rhine

Physical anthropologists derive their professional existence in part from the fact that human variability exists. It should be clear that at least a portion of the variability we assess is the result of genetic drift in small populations as well as adaptation to a large number of highly varied microenvironments across the world. Selection and drift thus work over the course of thousands of years to produce patterns of variability which may be compared and contrasted. Among the most readily assessed variants is morphology, which may be evaluated skeletally. As a consequence, the skeleton may be evaluated in the interest of discovering patterns of human variability.

Encapsulation of skeletal variability has traditionally been in terms of race. Contemporary physical anthropologists tend to see such studies as "old-fashioned" and not as interesting or useful as genetic variability determined from body chemistry. Moreover, there is a fear that the mantle of "racist" will settle upon anyone unwise enough to perform such studies. Perhaps there is also an underlying fear that, in the discovery of differences among peoples, one may provide ammunition to those outside of anthropology who wildly leap from differences to unwarranted conclusions about superiority or inferiority. This, of course, is nonsense. One should at least wistfully entertain the hope that society at the cusp of the 21st century would have progressed beyond the petty aspersions of racism to the recognition that, as with any species, our survival depends upon diversity.

There is, to be sure, always a danger that scientific data and conclusions might be wrenched from their context and that falsity and misinterpretation—intentional or otherwise—may result. But the forensic anthropologist has a very practical interest in race as an expression of biological difference and as a means of further describing some of the systematic human variability that does exist in order to apply those findings in a medicolegal context.

## Forensic Anthropology and Race

Forensic anthropology is that branch of physical anthropology that brings knowledge of the skeleton to bear upon medicolegal matters. It can therefore be regarded as a type of applied anthropology. The forensic anthropologist works with the medical and legal investigative systems and must describe human variability in such a way as to be understood by the general public, law enforcement officials, and even physicians. As Stewart (1979) observes: "from the standpoint of forensic anthropology, it is necessary to categorize the skeletal remains of unknowns in terms that reflect racial reality as it is locally understood." The forensic anthropologist who can tell officials that an unknown skull is, for instance, Hispanic, provides a datum useful in narrowing search parameters. By contrast, the forensic anthropologist who delivers a philosophical lecture to the sheriff on the nonexistence of human races is unlikely to be consulted again. This is indeed a very practical matter in applied anthropology.

The average forensic anthropologist does not deal with either the volume or the incompleteness of remains analyzed for the U.S. Army's Central Identification Laboratory by some of the contributors to this publication. Yet, remains are seldom complete. It is therefore necessary to continue to develop methods for racial attribution (and other properties) using criteria that may be evaluated when the clearest and most commonly employed indicators are absent.

## Skeletal Criteria

Over the years, it has been generally agreed that the skull (particularly the face) offers the surest and most positive means for evaluating the race of a subject. However, the skull may not be present, or the face may be too damaged to permit a full assessment. As a consequence, attention to other areas of the skull and the postcranium may offer further means of establishing the population to which the subject of an investigation belongs.

The purpose of this article is to present some of the criteria developed by a regional group of forensic anthropologists. This group, the Mountain Desert & Coastal Forensic Anthropologists, consists of the forensic anthropologists and their students living in the western United States. Beginning with our first meeting in 1981, several sessions were devoted to the topic of skeletal racial variability.

Our focus was on the four groups that constituted the major population strains in our region: Caucasoids, Mongoloids (Amerinds), Hispanics, and blacks. Other groups of increasing importance to forensic anthropologists as their numbers increase in the United States, such as Asians, were not included for lack of data. Clearly, much remains to be done.

Many of us were using a number of the classic traits found on the "Harvard List" of E. A. Hooton (Brues 1990). This is also the source of many of the features found in Bass (1987). Other traits were identified by various members of our group. Some are metric, but most are not. Some have been rigorously tested, while others have been subjected to only limited testing. Still others are the result of systematic observations that have not yet been fully quantified.

Many of the skull traits are bipolar—that is, they differentiate between two of the groups—but cannot be used to distinguish among them all. This, in part, accounts for the rather long list of characters evaluated. Moreover, continuously variable traits have ranges of overlap so that any meaningful evaluation must include a large number of traits.

## Nonmetric Traits

### *Caucasoids*

Caucasoids may be said in general to have a pointed, hatchet-faced look, as if they had evolved in a wind tunnel. The most productive area for racial evaluation, as Brues has noted (1990), is the midfacial region. As will be discussed below, Gill et al. (1988) have applied that observation metrically to the midface, and further quantification of this has been demonstrated by Curran (1990) and by Gill and Gilbert (1990).

Figure 1 illustrates a number of Caucasoid facial features. The nasion is deeply depressed and the nasal bones are "steepled" (Brues 1990). The intermaxillary suture contour more closely approximates vertical. The zygomatics slope back. The chin is strongly developed, with a tendency toward bilobateness in males and pointedness in females. There is a narrow nasal aperture, a deep sill, and a long spine. These combine to produce a long, narrow, high-relief nose. There are sloped "aviator glasses" orbits and a recurved zygomaticomaxillary suture as defined by Martindale (Gill 1986; Martindale and Gilbert 1984).

Figure 2 provides a lateral view of the skull to illustrate the undulation of the lower mandibular border, with a definite reduction in height at about M2. The ascending ramus tends to slope and is narrowed or "pinched in" midway. The oval window of the middle ear is visible (Napoli and Birkby 1990). An inion hook is often present on males. Although not shown clearly in this figure, there is a rather simple sutural pattern, typically lacking in sutural bones.

Figure 3 illustrates the long base chord. Note also the jagged form of the palatal suture and the elliptic form of the dental arcade (Gill 1986). Carabelli's cusps may be present (Hinkes 1990).

In addition to cranial and facial features, the cross section of the proximal femoral shaft approaches circularity in most Caucasoids (Gilbert and Gill 1990), and the femoral shaft is typically somewhat bowed in an anterior-posterior plane (Stewart 1979).

### *Mongoloids*

In this geographic context, Mongoloid must be understood as Amerind and indeed what follows is most common on recent prehistoric-to-contact-era indigenous southwestern populations. Long-headed Plains groups, particularly early ones, display more traits usually thought of as Caucasoid. But, in general, all may be said to have rounder, fuller, smoother

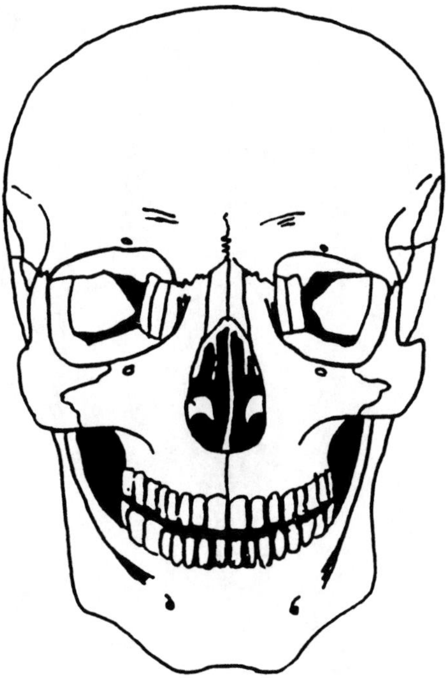

Figure 1. Caucasoid face, frontal view.

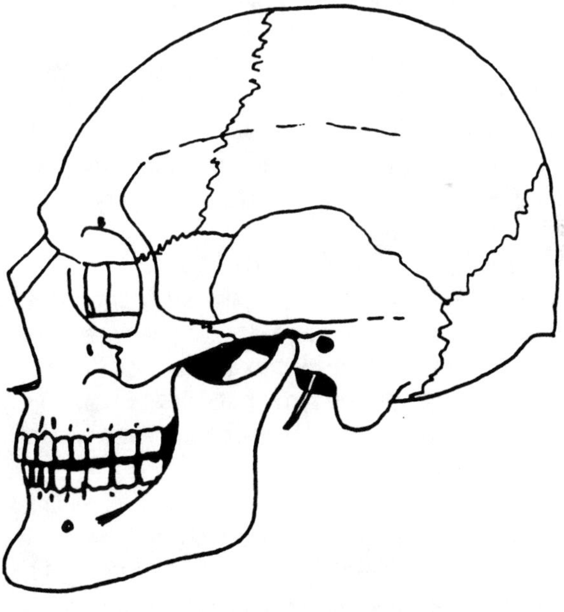

Figure 2. Caucasoid skull, lateral view.

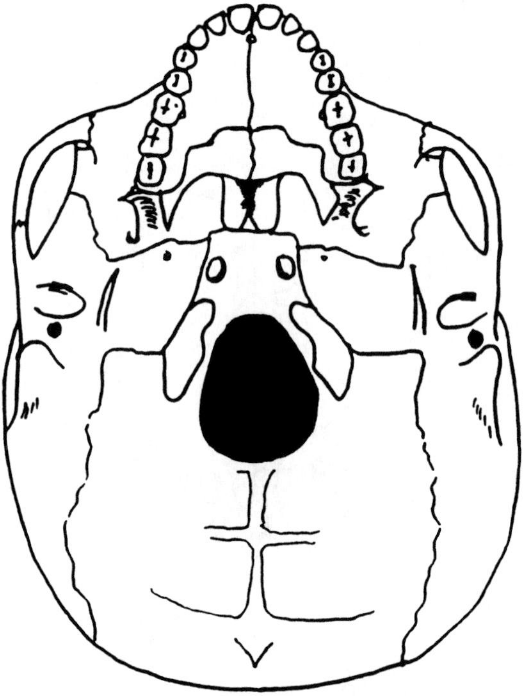

Figure 3. Caucasoid skull, basal view.

faces—more prominent zygomatics, often called "high cheekbones." The skull tends more toward brachycrania.

Figure 4 shows that the nasion is not deeply depressed and is often quite flat (Brues 1990). The intermaxillary contour is slightly concavoconvex below the small spine. American groups do vary in maxillary depth while maintaining the same general contour. A very similar contour is seen in the southeastern Pacific Non Nok Tha (Brooks et al. 1990). The zygomatics are quite vertical. As a consequence, the eyes appear to be more forwardly oriented in contrast to the more deeply set eyes of the Caucasoid. This flatness is revealed by Woo's Index (Woo and Morant 1934) and is shown even more clearly with the simometer (Gill et al. 1988). The nasal bones often show an "overgrowth," a projection inferiorly a millimeter or so into the nasal aperture.

The nasal bones are "tented"; they have a low relief profile (Brues 1990), and the frontal processes of the maxillae are "forward facing" as described by Gill and Gilbert (1990). The nasal aperture is of medium width and the sill blurred or indistinct. In prehistoric southwestern populations, the lower border is sometimes guttered. The spine is short. The orbits are

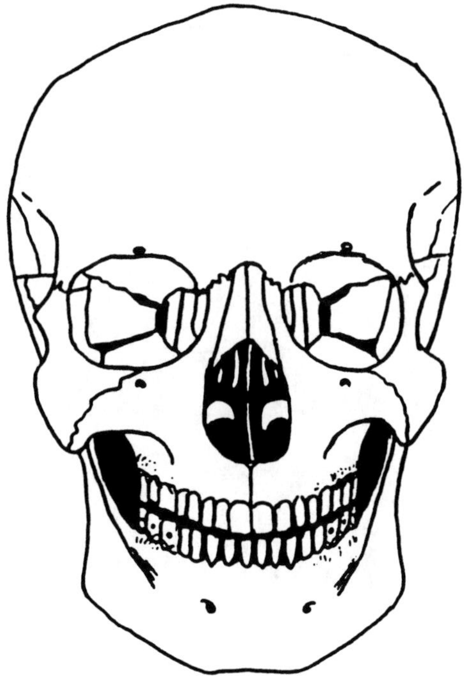

Figure 4. Mongoloid face, frontal view.

square to rounded. The zygomaticomaxillary suture is angled (Gill 1986; Martindale and Gilbert 1984), and there is an inferior zygomatic projection.

Figure 5 shows the more brachycephalic form of the skull. The oval window is not visible (Napoli and Birkby 1990). There are enamel extensions on the upper molars, along with buccal pits. The chin is more rounded and more blunt, the lower mandibular border is straight, the ascending ramus more nearly vertical, and with anterior and posterior borders more nearly parallel with little midramal pinching. The vault sutures, though not fully visible in this view, are more complex and often include sutural bones, particularly in the lambdoid suture.

Figure 6 reveals a short base chord. That is, the basion-opisthocranion distance is shorter in proportion to the opistocranion-prosthion distance than that seen in either blacks or whites. The flattening of the occiput seen in cradleboarded skulls accentuates this characteristic. The palatal suture is straight and the dental arcade is parabolic (Gill 1986). The incisors are typically shoveled (Dahlberg 1951; Hinkes 1990; Steele and Bramblett 1988), and the central incisors are medially rotated.

In cross section, the subtrochanteric femoral shaft is flattened anteroposteriorly (Gilbert and Gill 1990). The femoral shaft has relatively little anterior-posterior bowing.

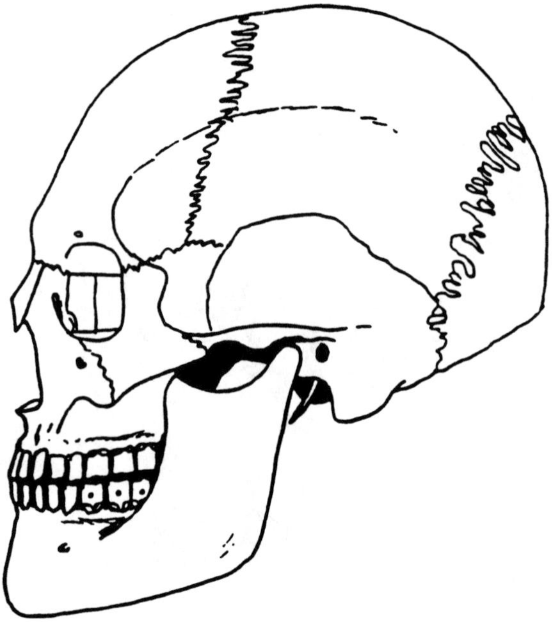

Figure 5. Mongoloid skull, lateral view.

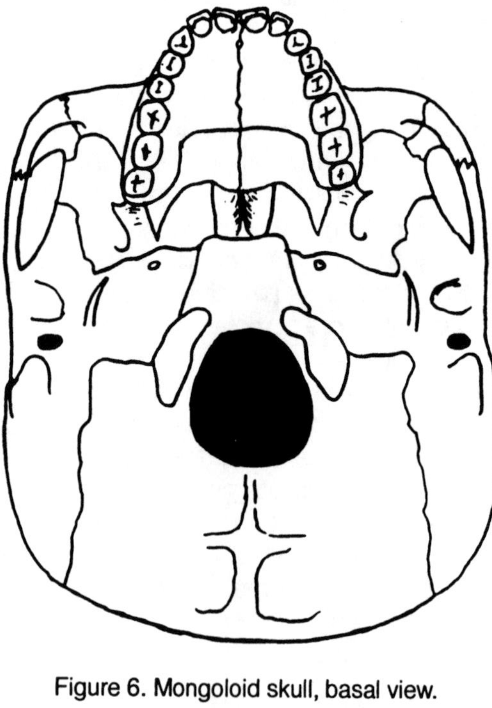

Figure 6. Mongoloid skull, basal view.

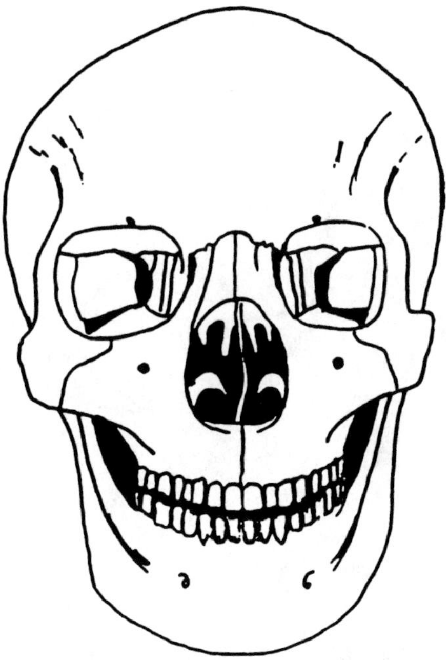

Figure 7. Negroid face, frontal view.

*Blacks*

This group, being more poorly represented in our regional skeletal sample, is less fully described. Figure 7 shows a moderate depression of the nasion and the "Quonset hut" morphology of the nasal bones: a wide, low curve from side to side (Brues 1990). The nasal aperture is typically of great width, with a guttered inferior margin with no sill. The spine is very small. The orbits are rectangular. The zygomaticomaxillary suture is somewhat recurved (Martindale and Gilbert 1984). The simometer shows the midface to be nonprojecting (Gill and Gilbert 1990).

Figure 8 shows the "paedomorphic" form of the skull (Krogman and Iscan 1986), generally smooth, with a rounded forehead and prominent occiput. There is a postbregmatic depression. There is commonly a "stepped" mastoid process (Gill 1986). Most individuals display considerable alveolar prognathism, with some showing a slight concavity beneath the inferior margin of the nasal aperture, while others show a more uniform slant. As many as 20 percent showed a contour more similar to whites, perhaps indicative of greater admixture (Brooks et al. 1990). Venous markings on the frontal are common. The oval window seems to be visible, but more extensive data remain to be gathered on this point. The chin tends to be somewhat retreating. The mandible is deep, the ascending rami are slightly

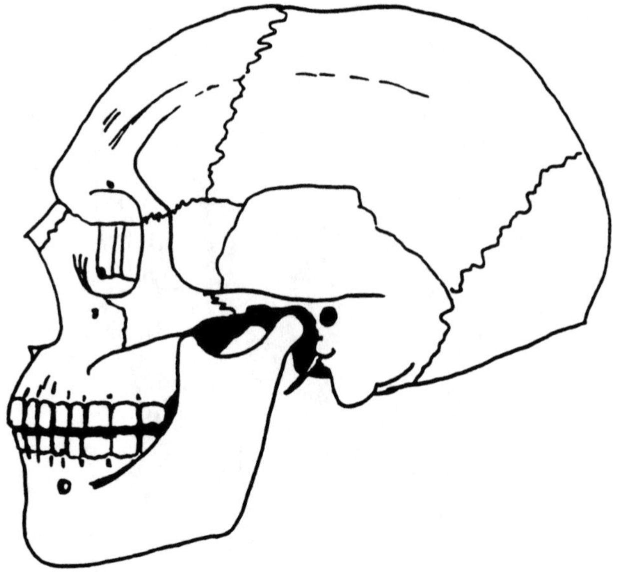

Figure 8. Negroid skull, lateral view.

pinched, and some lower margin undulation is common. As with whites, the suture pattern of blacks is simple and usually without sutural bones.

Figure 9 shows the long base chord. The palatal suture bulges and the dental arcade is hyperbolic (Gill 1986). Crenulation of molars is typical.

We have no data on the anterior femur cross section, but Stewart (1979) notes that the shaft is more flattened anteroposteriorly in midshaft, has less anterior torsion of the head and neck, and less anterior curvature than whites.

## Metric Assessment of Variability

Giles and Elliot's discriminant function race formula (1962) used an Indian Knoll prehistoric population as its Mongoloid data base and has stood the test of time surprisingly well, despite the fact that it does not properly classify those Indian populations not included in the original sample. It has been found to misclassify a large percentage of both southwestern (Birkby 1966) and Plains Indians (Fisher et al. 1984; Fisher and Gill 1990). Thus, while this formula cannot handle the full range of Amerind variability, Ayers et al. (1990) have found that by changing the Giles and Elliot black/white sectioning point from 89.27 to 62.89, the average correct placement for blacks and whites improves from 66.2 percent to 74.1 percent.

In a series of papers, Gill has refined the employment of one of the specialized coordinate calipers used by Howells (1973), the simometer, to

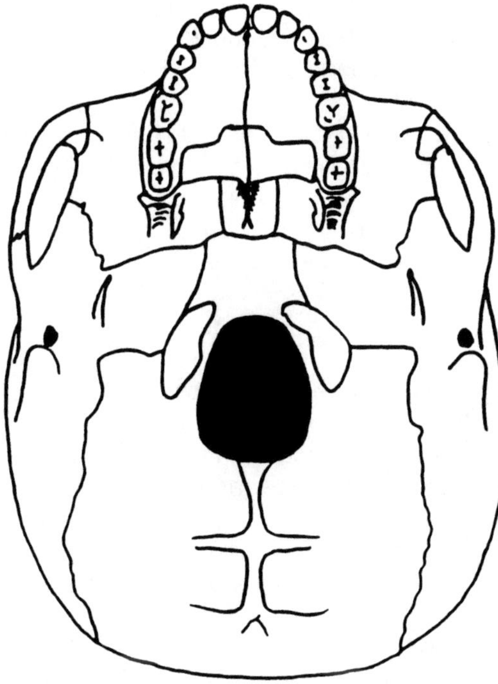

Figure 9. Negroid skull, basal view.

measure three upper facial chords (Gill 1984; Gill et al. 1988). These chords demonstrate even more clearly the Mongoloid facial flatness shown by Woo's index (Woo and Morant 1934) and, thus far, have distinguished clearly between Amerinds and Caucasoids. The three chords measured with the simometer correctly distinguish 85 percent of the more sharp-featured Caucasoids from all Amerind groups thus far tested (Curran 1990). The simometer also produces virtually the same values for blacks as Mongoloids, which serves to separate both of those groups from whites (Gilbert and Gill 1990).

By using only the intercondylar notch height of the femur, Baker et al. (1990) were able to correctly assess the race of males with accuracy varying between 66 percent and 88 percent. Where the race was known, the same measurement could be used to correctly identify the sex of between 76 percent and 82 percent of the sample.

Following up on an earlier study by Steele (1976), Pickering (1986) was able to correctly sort between 73 percent and 78 percent of a sample of male Southeast Asians and American Indians/Negroids/Caucasoids. He employed six measurements of the calcaneous, the same ones used previously by Steele to produce his discriminant functions.

As noted above, Gilbert and Gill also found that, by plotting the anterior-posterior versus mediolateral diameters of the femur against each other, between 78 percent and 85 percent of the sample of Amerinds and Caucasoids was correctly placed.

Using nine postcranial measurements in a discriminant function, Iscan and Cotton (1990) were able to correctly classify 94.9 percent of male and 90.7 percent of female blacks and whites. These samples came from the Hamann-Todd collection and included measurements of the innominate, femur, and tibia.

## Use of Documented Collections

Much of the data developed for assessing racial variability have been gathered from both the Terry and Hamman-Todd collections. Iscan (1990) has shown that, although individuals in the Terry Collection at the Smithsonian Institution were slightly larger and probably healthier than those in the Hamann-Todd collection at the Cleveland Museum of Natural History, they yield comparable results. Techniques for racial assessment from the pelvis were fairly successful for males but should be used only with great caution for females.

Unfortunately, both the Terry and the Hamman-Todd collections sample from a population that may have become somewhat outdated owing to well-documented secular trends that continue in contemporary populations. In an attempt to begin to update some of these data, Jantz and Moore-Jansen (1988) have assembled data on over 700 forensic specimens. This sample consists primarily of recent forensic cases and addresses, thereby, both metric and nonmetric variability in individuals born in this century. These forensic cases are drawn from 43 states and the District of Columbia. One cannot easily gather original data from this sample as one would with the Terry and Hamman-Todd collections. Nonetheless, the mass of data available makes it possible to approach many problems with fresh insight. Moreover, the new University of Tennessee FORDISC 1.0 computer program makes the use of incomplete specimens possible through custom discriminant function testing.

## Admixtures

Both American blacks and Hispanics may be regarded as admixtures of European stocks with native Africans and Native Americans. Dobzhansky (1962) has labeled both as "neoraces." However, the precise ancestral locus of any of the studied populations cannot be fixed. That is, the category here identified as Hispanic, for example, may be considered to be admixtures of various unknown (mostly) European groups with various unknown (mostly) American strains. Consequently, southwestern Hispanics may be different in important morphological details from, say, Cubans.

In deciding whether a particular skull should be identified as Hispanic, one would expect a large number of traits considered to be indications of both Caucasoid and Mongoloid to be found. A single trait labeled as Caucasoid, for example, in an otherwise Mongoloid skull would not suffice to identify it as Hispanic. As a rule of thumb, no fewer than a third of the menu of traits evaluated on a given skull should be accepted as adequate evidence for one to propose admixture.

Although a systematic evaluation has not been undertaken, individuals identified as Hispanic have shown a wide variety in the way in which traits considered as Caucasoid combine with those associated with Mongoloid. Hispanics display many features scored as Caucasoid, such as a long base chord, simple vault sutures, canine fossae, bilobate chin, prominent chin, mandibular undulation, pinched and slanted ascending ramus, and bulging palatal suture. On the other hand, features considered to be Mongoloid appearing with high frequency in Hispanics include a medium width of nasal aperture, minimal depression at nasion, a small nasal spine, a somewhat blurred sill, enamel extensions and buccal pits on at least some molars, and an elliptic dental arcade (Rhine 1990). However, individual skulls vary greatly from this general portrait.

## Conclusions

Both metric and nonmetric evaluations of skeletal morphology have been shown to be useful in the attribution of race. The attributions made can be recognized and employed by law enforcement and investigator personnel in forwarding their search for the identification of an unknown body. Recently, a comparison was made between attributed race of "John and Jane Doe" skeletons discovered in New Mexico between 1986 and 1991, and the actual race of those for whom an identity has been confirmed. To date, while 31 individuals remain unidentified, 39 have been positively identified. In every case, the attributed race, based on the traits discussed here, matched the actual race of the individual. Whether a possible misattribution of race may be a contributing factor to the inability to identify the remainder cannot be determined.

The success of the identification of an unknown body rests partly upon the initial anthropological assessment of the skeleton. Clearly, the attribution of sex, age, and race all contribute to the likelihood of a match being found. Not to attribute race decreases the probability of a match and thus works counter to the goal of the forensic anthropologist.

*Acknowledgments.* The kind invitation to participate in the American Anthropological Association's session on applied physical anthropology organized by Claire Gordon and Thomas Greiner provided the inspiration for the oral presentation upon which this article is based. George Gill thoughtfully read and commented on a late draft of the article, which incorporates many of his suggestions. Thanks are also due to the many contributors to the volume on skeletal race attribution (Gill and Rhine 1990), which has provided the basis for much of the material presented here.

## References Cited

Ayers, H. G., R. L. Jantz, and P. H. Moore-Jansen
1990 Giles and Elliot Race Discriminant Functions Revisited: A Test Using Recent Forensic Cases. *In* Skeletal Attribution of Race. G. W. Gill and S. Rhine, eds. Albuquerque, NM: Maxwell Museum of Anthropology, Anthropological Papers No. 4.
Baker, S. J., G. W. Gill, and D. A. Kieffer
1990 Race and Sex Determination from the Intercondylar Notch of the Femur. *In* Skeletal Attribution of Race. G. W. Gill and S. Rhine, eds. Albuquerque, NM: Maxwell Museum of Anthropology, Anthropological Papers No. 4.
Bass, W. M.
1987 Human Osteology. 3rd ed. Columbia: Missouri Archaeological Society.
Birkby, W. H.
1966 An Evaluation of Race and Sex Identification from Cranial Measurements. American Journal of Physical Anthropology 24:21–28.
Brooks, S., R. M. Brooks, and D. France
1990 Alveolar Prognathism Contour, An Aspect of Racial Identification. *In* Skeletal Attribution of Race. G. W. Gill and S. Rhine, eds. Albuquerque, MN: Maxwell Museum of Anthropology, Anthropological Papers No. 4.
Brues, A. M.
1990 The Once and Future Diagnosis of Race. *In* Skeletal Attribution of Race. G. W. Gill and S. Rhine, eds. Albuquerque, NM: Maxwell Museum of Anthroplogy, Anthropological Papers No. 4.
Curran, B. K.
1990 The Application of Measures of Midfacial Projection for Racial Classification. *In* Skeletal Attribution of Race. G. W. Gill and S. Rhine, eds. Maxwell Museum of Anthropology, Anthropological Papers No. 4.
Dahlberg, A. A.
1951 The Dentition of the American Indian. *In* The Physical Anthropology of the American Indian. W. S. Laughlin, ed. New York: Viking Fund Publications in Anthropology.
Dobzhansky, Theodosius
1962 Mankind Evolving. New Haven, CT: Yale University Press.
Fisher, T. D., G. W. Gill, and P. D. Lanum
1984 Application of the Giles-Elliot Discriminant Function Formulae to a Cranial Sample of Northwestern Plains Indians. Paper presented at American Academy of Forensic Sciences, Anaheim.
Fisher, T. D., and G. W. Gill
1990 Application of the Giles and Elliot Discriminant Function Formulae to a Cranial Sample of Northwestern Plains Indians. *In* Skeletal Attribution of Race. G. W. Gill and S. Rhine, eds. Maxwell Museum of Anthropology, Anthropological Papers No. 4.
Gilbert, R., and G. W. Gill
1990 A Metric Technique for Identifying American Indian Femora. *In* Skeletal Attribution of Race. G. W. Gill and S. Rhine, eds. Maxwell Museum of Anthropology, Anthropological Papers No. 4.
Giles, E., and O. Elliot
1962 Race Identification from Cranial Measurements. Journal of Forensic Sciences 7:147–156.
Gill, G. W.
1984 A Forensic Test Case for a New Method of Geographical Race Determination. *In* Human Identification: Case Studies in Forensic Anthropology. T. A. Rathbun and J. E. Buikstra, eds. Springfield, IL: Charles C Thomas.
1986 Craniofacial Criteria in Forensic Race Identification. *In* Forensic Osteology: Advances in the Identification of Human Remains. Springfield, IL: Charles C Thomas.
Gill, G. W., S. S. Hughes, S. M. Bennett, and B. M. Gilbert
1988 Racial Identification from the Midfacial Skeleton with Special Reference to American Indians and Whites. Journal of Forensic Sciences 13:92–99.
Gill, G. W., and B. M. Gilbert
1990 Race Identification from the Midfacial Skeleton: American Blacks and Whites. *In* Skeletal Attribution of Race. G. W Gill and S. Rhine, eds. Albuquerque, NM: Maxwell Museum of Anthropology, Anthropological Papers No. 4.

Hinkes, M. J.
1990 Shovel Shaped Incisors in Human Identification. *In* Skeletal Attribution of Race. G. W. Gill and S. Rhine, eds. Albuquerque, NM: Maxwell Museum of Anthropology, Anthropological Papers No. 4.
Howells, W. W.
1973 Cranial Variation in Man. Papers of the Peabody Museum of Archaeology and Ethnology, Harvard University, Cambridge, MA.
Iscan, M. Y.
1990 A Comparison of Techniques on the Determination of Race, Sex and Stature from the Terry and Hamann-Todd Collections. *In* Skeletal Attribution of Race. G. W. Gill and S. Rhine, eds. Albuquerque, NM: Maxwell Museum of Anthropology, Anthropological Papers No. 4.
Iscan, M. Y., and T. S. Cotton
1990 Osteometric Assessment of Racial Affinity from Multiple Sites in the Postcranial Skeleton. *In* Skeletal Attribution of Race. G. W. Gill and S. Rhine, eds. Albuquerque, NM: Maxwell Museum of Anthropology, Anthropological Papers No. 4.
Jantz, R. L., and P. H. Moore-Jansen
1988 A Data Base for Forensic Anthropology: Structure, Content and Analysis. Department of Anthropology Report of Investigations No. 47, University of Tennessee.
Krogman, W. M., and M. Y. Iscan
1986 The Human Skeleton in Forensic Medicine. 2nd ed. Springfield, IL: Charles C Thomas.
Martindale, S. W., and B. M. Gilbert
1984 Race Determination from Cranio-facial Variation in American Indians and Whites. Paper presented at American Academy of Forensic Sciences Meeting, Anaheim.
Napoli, M., and W. H. Birkby
1990 Racial Differences in the Visibility of the Oval Window in the Middle Ear. *In* Skeletal Attribution of Race. G. W. Gill and S. Rhine, eds. Albuquerque, NM: Maxwell Museum of Anthropology, Anthropological Papers No. 4.
Pickering, R. B.
1986 Population Differences in the Calcaneous as Determined by Discriminant Function Analysis. *In* Forensic Osteology: Advances in the Identification of Human Remains. Springfield, IL: Charles C Thomas.
Rhine, Stanley
1990 Non-Metric Skull Racing. *In* Skeletal Attribution of Race. G. W. Gill and S. Rhine, eds. Albuquerque, NM: Maxwell Museum of Anthropology, Anthropological Papers No. 4.
Steele, D. G.
1976 The Estimation of Sex on the Basis of the Talus and Calcaneous. American Journal of Physical Anthropology 45:581–588.
Steele, D. G., and C. A. Bramblett
1988 The Anatomy and Biology of the Human Skeleton. College Station: Texas A & M Press.
Stewart, T. D.
1979 Essentials of Forensic Anthropology. Springfield, IL: Charles C Thomas.
Woo, T. L., and G. M. Morant
1934 A Biometric Study of "Flatness" of the Facial Skeleton in Man. Biometrika 16:196–250.

# Dental Variation and Racial Estimation: Problems and Practical Forensic Applications

Kim Schneider Kimminau

There is a need for racial estimation in the context of forensic identification, and studies of race have a long history within American physical anthropology. The discipline was shaped largely by two individuals, Earnest Albert Hooton and Ales Hrdlicka, both of whom had strongly held beliefs in the "reality" of race. These individuals, who launched the careers of many important anthropologists, were trained in what has been called 'the white-man's burden' strain of elitism largely affected by the racism in the ethos of French anthropology (Brace 1982).

Concepts of race do not appear to have been much affected by the synthetic theory of evolution that had such a major impact on biological science in general (Mayr and Provine 1980). A population-level approach to the study of human variation did not develop quickly. Rather, the concept of race remained insulated and was linked frequently with biological determinism. It has only been in the recent past that the discipline has begun to actively struggle with the concept of race as it applies to skeletal variation.

One of the principal reasons that the concept of race has recently reappeared in book titles, journal articles, and research papers is that there have been many developments in the subdisciplines of applied and forensic anthropology. The growth of these subdisciplines has been due to the increased application of anthropological expertise to areas outside the realm of academics. Support provided by medical examiners' offices for example, has promoted the development of many useful techniques and applications for anthropological skills. It is within this milieu that a renewed interest in refining and/or redefining racial variation has grown. Practical situations may require that anthropologists make determinations of race or establish parameters for categorizing the biological populations with which they work.

## Skeletal Attributes of Race

Skeletal biologists have developed a battery of discrete and metric features that are useful in the identification of "major" racial groups. Each of these researchers would certainly agree that no single feature is all-encompassing or "key" to racial assessment. Racial estimation improves when the suite of features is broad. Skeletal indicators that have proved most useful include: contour of the nasal root (Brues 1990), cranial discrete traits

(Napoli and Birkby 1990; Rhine 1990), facial shape (Brooks et al. 1990; Gill and Gilbert 1990; Howells 1973), craniometrics (Giles and Elliot 1962), and mandibular ramus inversion (Angel and Kelley 1990). Some of these researchers have maintained a population-specific focus, much like that maintained in the development of stature estimation formulae, that has enabled them to document variation within relatively small samples and extrapolate to larger populations by comparison. Others have focused on "the Big Three" mega-populations, which includes Negroids, Mongoloids, and Caucasoids, or they have variably sectioned these three groups into smaller units. Both of these research preferences have promoted broader-scaled comparisons utilizing an increasingly large battery of traits recognized as useful in racial identification.

## Dental Attributes of Race

Features of the dentition also have been used in racial assessment. While the subdiscipline of dental anthropology is relatively new, researchers have long recognized that discrete traits of teeth, odontometrics, and dental histology vary among human populations. Although virtually every student of osteology is aware of dental variants, the use of dental features in the assessment of race has received less attention than that of skeletal indicators. The most obvious exceptions to this trend include the works of Dahlberg (1963), Hrdlicka (shovel-shaped incisors) (1920), Lasker and Lee (1957), and Jacobson (South African Negroes) (1982). Perhaps the most influential researcher recently has been Christy Turner who, since 1967, has been documenting racial variation in dentition on a worldwide scale. This effort has not yet been matched in the arena of skeletal biology as it applies to racial identification.

There exist a number of advantages in using dental attributes in the process of racial estimation. The dental shape, size, and presence or absence of discrete traits of the dentition apparently are quite stable genetically, and they are not likely to be influenced strongly by developmental or environmental perturbations during formation (Eisenmann 1980). Furthermore, the likelihood of intact dental specimens being present in a forensic context is usually quite high. Teeth are relatively protected in the oral cavity and may survive high impact trauma or fire, for example, better than other portions of the body. The number and variety of teeth in the adult dentition allow for a large number of traits to be observed quickly, and speed is often a factor in forensic cases. Finally, the effect(s) of dentistry and the availability of antemortem radiographs may allow for "easy" forensic identification even in cases where racial assessment is not possible (and by extension, is not required).

The presence or absence of Carabelli's complex on maxillary first molars and shovel-shaped maxillary central incisors probably are the most commonly used dental features associated with dental analysis. While these characteristics are useful, they are not enough to make a realistic forensic racial estimation. Researchers may use these traits dogmatically without regard to the balance of dentition present in the remains. Just as is the case for discrete trait analysis in cranial and infracranial material, so it is that these two specific features must be used with caution and tempered by a broader vision of racial assessment. For example, Turner's work with Mongoloid dentitions from throughout Asia and the Pacific documents that there are eight diagnostic morphological traits that distinguish Sundadonts (South Asians, Japanese (Jomon), and Australians) from Sinodonts (Chinese, Northeast Asians [except recent Russians], and Native Americans). These features include shovel- and double-shovel-shaped maxillary central incisors but also include one-rooted maxillary anterior premolars, enamel extensions on maxillary first molars, reduced, peg-shaped, or congenitally absent maxillary third molars, deflecting wrinkles on mandibular first molars and four-cusped mandibular second molars (Turner 1990). Unlike many discrete traits used in skeletal material, which are either present or absent, many dental discrete traits vary on a continuum of expression. This feature requires ascribing arbitrary grades within each character sequence. Such grading systems do not presume a genetic component to each grade; rather, the recognition of variability within each feature allows only for comparable scoring of features among researchers (Dahlberg 1971).

Other features of teeth that are useful in estimating racial affinity include dental size and intraclass proportion differences (Kieser 1990). General trends include relatively large anterior teeth as compared to posterior teeth among Asian Mongoloids as compared to Native Americans. Caucasoids tend to have relatively small maxillary lateral incisors as compared to maxillary central incisors, and the congenital absence of maxillary lateral incisors occurs in 5 to 10 percent of all human populations, except among Negroids (Dahlberg 1951). Cusp number and groove complexity varies among these groups. For example, Caucasoids tend to display relatively complex molar surfaces while Negroids and Mongoloids do not typically have elaborated occlusal surfaces.

## Forensic Application

Traditional forensic dental identification rests almost exclusively on radiographic and/or dental records comparison using dental restorative patterns without regard to dental morphology. Due to increased community water fluoridation programs, better dental prophylactics, and increased public awareness of the importance of dental hygiene, many contemporary groups are caries-free (Bowen 1991). The results of the National Institute of Health's survey of oral health (1988) document that between 2.7 and 4.1 percent of adults between the ages of 18 and 64 years do not have any caries in the dentition.

In addition, the number of decayed or filled surface restorations (DFSR) for this age group varies between 0.6 to 1.03 per person. A low rate of restoration further suggests that, while there is regional variation, younger individuals are less likely to have dental fillings and would therefore be more difficult to identify dentally in a forensic context. However, caries prevalence rises with age. For example, the highest prevalence of decayed or filled surfaces (31 DFS) was observed in people between 45 and 49 years of age. This pattern highlights the difficulty of applying traditional antemortem/postmortem dental radiographic identification for certain groups of contemporary populations. Given such an epidemiological trend, the recognition of dental morphological features useful for racial estimation becomes all the more important.

Another difficulty in using teeth for racial estimation is that individuals of mixed racial ancestry may display dental (and skeletal) features common to both parental heritages. Although little is published on this issue, forensic anthropologists generally can distinguish the racial ancestries represented by the "mixed messages" observed in the skeletal features routinely used. Teeth can be used to validate such observations. In a recent case, eroded remains were repatriated from Southeast Asia alleged to be those of a U.S. serviceman killed in a firefight during the Vietnam War. The remains consisted of seven incomplete long bones and most of the skull and mandible. Due to the incomplete nature of the infracranial remains, few standard anthropological estimations could be made, and racial estimation rested solely on the reconstructed facial and dental features. While the nasal, midfacial, and malar portions of the skull appeared most consistent with Mongoloid ancestry, the presence of a weak nasal gutter and the shape of the mandible and dental arcades were more consistent with Negroid ancestry.

The dental evidence of this case consisted of the maxillae with 11 teeth and the mandible with 12 teeth. None of the teeth displayed any restorative dentistry although clinical caries were present on all four first molars. The anterior dentition, particularly the maxillary incisors and premolars, displayed characteristics of Sinodonty while the posterior teeth displayed features more commonly observed in Negroids rather than Mongoloids. This apparent "mixture" of racial features mirrored that observed in the bony remains.

Based on a combination of circumstantial information and the exclusion of other fatalities in the proximity of the incident of the alleged fatality, an identification recommendation was made. The individual who best matched the biological profile established for the remains was listed as "Negro" on his official military medical and dental records. An antemortem photograph of the individual was used in a cranial superimposition that further corroborated the identification. An examination of the antemortem photograph revealed that the individual did not display phenotypic features generally associated with individuals of sub-Saharan descent; rather the individual appeared to share features in common with Mongoloid or possibly Caucasoid ancestries. Since the acceptance of the identification of these remains, the family stated that they were originally from the West Indies and are of mixed Indian and Black/Carib racial heritages.

## Summary and Conclusions

As forensic cases continue to reflect the growing pattern of decreased caries and dental restorations among younger age groups in the United States, a growing interest must develop in recognizing racial features present in dentition. The coordinated effort of forensic odontologists and anthropologists can improve racial estimation, which may provide a substantive basis for identification. Both disciplines can benefit from expanding their perspectives by using various morphologic features as part of their forensic analyses.

## References Cited

Angel, J. L., and J. O. Kelley
1990 Inversion of the Posterior Edge of the Jaw Ramus: New Race Trait. *In* Skeletal Attribution of Race. G. W. Gill and S. Rhine, eds. Pp. 27–32. Albuquerque, NM: Maxwell Museum of Anthropology, Anthropological Papers No. 4.

Bowen, W. H.
1991 Dental Caries: Is It an Extinct Disease? Journal of the American Dental Association 122:49–52.

Brace, C. L.
1982 The Roots of the Race Concept in American Physical Anthropology. *In* A History of American Physical Anthropology 1930–1980. F. Spencer, ed. Pp. 11–29. New York: Academic Press.

Brooks, S., R. H. Brooks, and D. France
1990 Alveolar Prognathism Contour, an Aspect of Racial Identification. *In* Skeletal Attribution of Race. G. W. Gill and S. Rhine, eds. Pp. 41–46. Albuquerque, NM: Maxwell Museum of Anthropology, Anthropological Papers No. 4.

Brues, A.
1990 The Once and Future Diagnosis of Race. *In* Skeletal Attribution of Race. G. W. Gill and S. Rhine, eds. Pp. 1–7. Albuquerque, NM: Maxwell Museum of Anthropology, Anthropological Papers No. 4.

Dahlberg, A. A.
1951 The Dentition of the American Indian. *In* The Physical Anthropology of the American Indian. W. S. Laughlin, ed. Pp. 138–176. New York: Viking Fund.
1963 Analysis of the American Indian Dentition. *In* Dental Anthropology. D. R. Brothwell, ed. Pp. 149–178. Oxford: Pergamon Press.
1971 Penetrance and Expressivity of Dental Traits. *In* Dental Morphology and Evolution. A. A. Dahlberg, ed. Pp. 257–262. Chicago, IL: University of Chicago Press.

Eisenmann, D. R.
1980 Amelogenesis. *In* Oral Histology: Development, Structure, and Function. A. R. Tencate, ed. Pp. 182–193. St. Louis, MO: C. V. Mosby.

Giles, E., and O. Elliot
1962 Race Identification from Cranial Measurements. Journal of Forensic Sciences 7:147–157.

Gill, G. W., and B. M. Gilbert
1990 Race Identification from the Midfacial Skeleton: American Blacks and Whites. *In* Skeletal Attribution of Race. G. W. Gill and S. Rhine, eds. Pp. 47–53. Albuquerque, NM: Maxwell Museum of Anthropology, Anthropological Papers No. 4.

Howells, W. W.
1973 Cranial Variation in Man. Peabody Museum Papers, 67. Boston, MA: Peabody Museum.
Hrdlicka, A.
1920 Shovel-Shaped Teeth. American Journal of Physical Anthropology 3:429–465.
Jacobson, A.
1982 The Dentition of the South African Negro. Anniston, AL: Higginbotham.
Kieser, J. A.
1990 Human Adult Odontometrics. Cambridge Studies in Biological Anthropology, 4. New York: Cambridge University Press.
Lasker, G. W., and M. M. C. Lee
1957 Racial Traits in the Human Teeth. Journal of Forensic Sciences 12:401–419.
Mayr, E., and W. B. Provine
1980 The Evolutionary Synthesis: Perspectives on the Unification of Biology. Cambridge, MA: Harvard University Press.
Napoli, M. L., and W. H. Birkby
1990 Racial Differences in the Oval Window in the Middle Ear. *In* Skeletal Attribution of Race. G. W. Gill and S. Rhine, eds. Pp. 27–32. Albuquerque, NM: Maxwell Museum of Anthropology, Anthropological Papers No. 4.
National Institutes of Health
1988 Oral Health of United States Adults. The National Survey of Oral Health in U.S. Employed Adults and Seniors: 1985–1987. Regional findings. NIH Publication no. 87-2869. Washington, DC: U.S. Government Printing Office.
Rhine, S.
1990 Non-Metric Skull Racing. *In* Skeletal Attribution of Race. G. W. Gill and S. Rhine, eds. Pp. 9–20. Albuquerque, NM: Maxwell Museum of Anthropology, Anthropological Papers No. 4.
Turner, C.
1990 Major Features of Sundadonty and Sinodonty, Including Suggestions about East Asian Microevolution, Population History, and Late Pleistocene Relationships with Australian Aboriginals. American Journal of Physical Anthropology 82:295–317.

# Racial Concepts

## The Objective View of Race

Alice M. Brues

I am beginning to understand how astronomers feel. The relation between the scientific study of regional differences in man, and racism, is similar to the relation between astronomy and astrology. Astronomy is an attempt to understand a portion of the universe: astrology is an attempt to convert certain parts of this information into a kind of divination, to predict the characteristics, behavior, or fortunes of human beings. But so far I have not heard of anybody trying to tell astronomers that they cannot use the words "star" or "planet" because to do so might seem to endorse the validity of the horoscopes in the daily paper.

It is a major function of the mind to try to find relations between things. A type of relation that promises to be particularly useful is that between the appearance of something and how that object, or person, will react in a future situation. The behavioral expectations inferred from the external appearance of an individual, including but not limited to genetically determined characters, are a good example. Unfortunately, the hope of finding relations that have practical value readily leads one optimistically to assume relations that are false or very tenuous; this is what most folklore consists of. Science has always been concerned as much with rejecting false relations as with finding true ones.

A basic problem with the definition of the word "race" is the confusion between the attributes of a given population that are genetic in nature versus those that are externally controlled or due to historic events. If the assumption is made that some of these attributes cause the others, or that they all are due to a single causal factor, we will expect them to remain together, continuing to appear in the same individuals from generation to generation. This satisfies the "folklore" generalization that if an individual looks thus-and-so, he will act in a predictable manner. It would be so convenient, if this were true, that people love to believe it. If everything about race is in one tight bundle, you can attach a convenient handle to it, perhaps a color word, and have no further strain on your brain.

It is perhaps as a result of this older idea of race being a correlated bundle of physical and behavioral characteristics, that we have a present disagreement between anthropologists about the use of the word. Physical anthropologists, in light of the overall hereditary nature once assumed for the whole bundle, are inclined to think that the word "race" should be retained for the elements that actually *are* hereditary. Some cultural anthropologists seem to feel that if the things they are primarily interested in are removed from the definition of race, it becomes a useless term and should be discarded.

Unfortunately, one of the earliest attempts to replace the word "race" was the suggestion by Ashley-Montagu that the phrase "ethnic group" be used as a substitute. This was not a newly coined term. It had been used earlier in connection with European immigration to the United States, and it was applied to nationalities or to smaller groups such as the Serbs and Croatians of the former Yugoslavia. Although Ashley Montagu was a physical anthropologist, he inadvertently reemphasized cultural and linguistic criteria by the use of the term "ethnic group," and thus, in my opinion, increased rather than eliminated confusion.

A second semantic problem lies in the degree to which categories (of race or anything else) are assumed to denote uniformity of type among individual specimens. Many people in the general public, including some we consider educated, are still struggling with words and statements in a manner that goes back to Plato and the 4th century B.C. Plato theorized that there existed, in a kind of heaven, an ideal model corresponding to every Greek noun, of which actual terrestrial examples were more or less imperfect copies. This theory implied that if things did not conform to type according to the class to which they were assigned, at least they *should,* and that the real world was inferior to the ideal world because of this individual variation. This normative function of the ideal type is wholly inappropriate to biological thinking, in which variation is as essential as similarity; or to statistical thinking, in which variation is itself a quantity subject to measurement. In any sexually reproducing organism, similarity of individuals in a population results from their drawing from the same gene pool according to the laws of probability, and differences between populations are a function of difference in the frequencies of various genes in their separate gene pools.

We could do better if all students, no later than the third grade, had been introduced to the idea that there are different kinds of statements: one kind of statement is "Men are taller than women" and another kind of statement is "Mary is taller than John"; and that it is because these are different kinds of statements that both can be true. At least, let's point this out in our college classrooms. Then our students might be better equipped to understand the nature of biological variation, which is precisely what we must understand to think, speak, and act realistically in regard to what we call race.

It is interesting that while English distinguishes the common noun (for a group) and the proper noun (for an individual) by capitalizing the proper noun, another widely spoken European language, German, capitalizes all nouns, thus de-emphasizing the distinction. Is there any subconscious influence here that causes a German-speaking person to think more rigidly about class designations, such as race? I leave that to our psychological anthropologists.

If we are to limit descriptions of race to inherited traits, we must turn to the history of the application of genetics to the human species, for the question of inheritance of racial characteristics was a matter of interest quite early on.

One of the earliest studies of Mendelian genetics in the human species involved racial differences and was done by Dr. C. B. Davenport of the Carnegie Institution in 1913. Studying a large population of individuals of known mixed white/black ancestry on the island of Jamaica, he showed by a simple table that in a population of uniform mixed ancestry, there was no correlation between skin color and hair form; that there were individuals with dark skin and straight hair, individuals with light skin and woolly hair; and that these and all other combinations occurred in exactly the numbers that would be expected if the two traits were inherited quite independently (see Figure 1).

Now Dr. Davenport was a racist according to the universal habit of his time. He believed that there were distinct differences, on the average, between the two parental races in functional capacities; but he immediately

*"II. Correlation Between Color of the Skin and Form of the Hair in the $F_2$ Generation.*

*The correlation surface is given in Table 34.*

Table 34.-Correlation between color of the skin and form of the hair.

| Medium Class Value<br>Skin Color | 6<br>0-11 | 18<br>12-25 | 33<br>26-40 | 48<br>41-55 | 63<br>56-70 | Total |
|---|---|---|---|---|---|---|
| Form of Hair: | | | | | | |
| 1 (straight) | | 4 | 5 | 2 | 1 | 12 |
| 2 (wavy) | | | 10 | 2 | | 12 |
| 3 (curly) | 2 | 8 | 15 | 1 | 1 | 27 |
| 4 (very curly) | | | 9 | 3 | | 12 |
| 5 (woolly) | 1 | | 3 | 4 | | 8 |
| Total | 3 | 12 | 42 | 12 | 2 | 71 |

N.B. - The tabular entries indicate the frequency with which the given correlation occurs.

*The correlation calculated from table 23 is + 0.043 ± 0.080. Expressed in English this means that there is no evidence of any correlation at all. An inspection of table 34 shows that one of the two extracted full black-skinned individuals had straight hair, and that one of the extracted white-skinned individuals had woolly hair. Black skin color and woolly hair are closely associated in the pure-bred negro, but the association is, so to say, accidental. The determiners for the two traits dissociate in the germ-cells of the hybrids and reappear in the next generation in all possible combinations."*

Figure 1. Independent assortment of skin color and hair form. (*Source:* C. B. Davenport, *Heredity of Skin Color in Negro-White Crosses.* Publication No. 188, p. 45. Washington, DC: Carnegie Institution of Washington, 1913.)

pointed out, correctly, that if two characteristic physical traits segregated in the Mendelian sense in the genetic process, other heritable characteristics would also, and that therefore it was not possible to infer an individual's intelligence or other functional characteristics from his physical traits: it had to be ascertained individually for each person. Thus, the idea of race as a combination of characteristics that were inherently associated and would be correlated forever was effectively "deconstructed" in 1913 by a geneticist who in some respects was still a 19th-century racist but who was, nevertheless, a scientist who understood the meaning of a zero correlation. Seventy-eight years later, many members of the general public have still not gotten the message.

So what is the present definition of race, as the biologist sees it? A race is a population that differs from others by the frequency of certain genes and the characteristics they produce. A more technical way of expressing it is to say that racially different populations have different gene pools. The existence of distinguishable gene pools within a species implies some mechanism of at least partial isolation, which in most cases is geographical in nature. The biologist's definition usually includes an estimate of the percentage of cases, overall, that can be assigned definitely to a particular subspecies if the division into subspecies is to be considered valid. Although all biologists do not use the same figure, 80 percent is commonly given. Interestingly, this is of the same order of magnitude as the precision with which a forensic anthropologist can assign an unknown skull to the population from which it actually comes. The nature of the subspecies, or race, is such that it does not have clear boundaries, except where a geographical barrier at a particular point is truly impassable; thus, no matter what kind of classification one uses, it is never possible to assign every individual to one and only one race, and whole populations may be transitional in phenotype. In the old, simplistic days, it was assumed that the farther back in history you went, the less ambiguity there was about racial groups, and that the present state of the species resulted from historical churning up of groups that at one time were more physically distinct from one another than they now are. In some cases this may be true, in other cases probably not.

The idea of races as watertight categories has been promoted by attempts, for a variety of motives, to make legal distinctions between races. At the beginning of the civil rights movement in the United States, it was quite logically proposed that all designations of race in public records should be expunged. Unfortunately, in a very short time the designations were restored, again for the best kind of motives, so that now in many cities every child entering the first grade has to be assigned to a "race" so that we know which school to bus him to. It is also, of course, necessary to tag people with race designations in order to verify affirmative action.

To come down to practical matters, nowadays it is not sufficient to try to find out what is true in the world. In many circles it is considered necessary to decide, independent of the truth, what to tell people. There have always been different kinds of truth. There is religious truth; you will go to hell if you do not believe it. There is political truth; society will go to hell if everybody does not believe it. The third kind of truth is real truth, which corresponds to some kind of external reality. The latter kind of truth is the only kind from which you can proceed by reasoned stages to a better understanding of the world around you, which may make it possible for you to change and hopefully improve that world. But religious and political truth give the promise of a quick fix. A popular political statement now is "There is no such thing as race." I wonder what people are going to think when they hear this. They would have to suppose that the speaker, if he were dropped by parachute into downtown Nairobi, would be unable to tell, by looking around him, whether he was in Nairobi or Stockholm. This could only damage his credibility. The visible differences between different populations of the world tell everyone that *there is something there*. We had better be prepared to explain what is there, and why, before we discuss what it does or does not mean.

Another problem with refusing to talk about race, except to deny its existence, is that young people, even quite small children, have a remarkable ability to sense when their elders have a hang-up about something. Their reaction is to drop the subject immediately and to go look for information elsewhere. In the days long past when sex, not race, was the great forbidden subject, people were warned that if they did not talk to their children about sex, they would go for information to "bad companions on the street corner." Now, when young people ask about "race" and see a look of panic on your face, they will simply fall back on folklore. That is not going to help matters. The alternative is to be prepared to discuss why different populations look different, which requires a knowledge of genetics and how a race or subspecies can be described, which requires a knowledge of biological variation in general, statistics, central tendencies, measures of variance, and the overlapping of distribution curves. Unfortunately, these are all things that our present precollege school systems usually ignore, which many students do not encounter even in college, and which some members of anthropology departments are not comfortable with either.

To look a little beyond the present to the upcoming future, the promotion of multiculturalism may complicate the picture. When minorities talk about themselves, we may find that their perception of their own identity involves physical and cultural elements bound up together as in the older idea of race. Then what will we tell them? Whatever we tell them, we may get involved in factionalism between traditionalists, modernists, and other elements *within* minority groups, further complicated by the generation gaps that every community has.

I, for one, propose to stick to biological reality, which is something solid to cling to amidst the changing winds of the political scene.

# Applied Anthropology and the Concept of Race: A Legacy of Linnaeus

Norman J. Sauer

Nearly two-and-one-half centuries ago, Carolus Linnaeus presented to the scientific community in his famous *Systemae Naturae* (Linnaeus 1757) a classification of human varieties. He listed four groups: *Europeaus* (*albus*), "white"; *Americanus* (*rufescens*), "red"; *Asiaticus* (*fuscus*), "dark"; and *Africanus* (*niger*), "black."

With later embellishment by Blumenbach, thus was born in a time of nascent exploration, in a time when scientists debated whether God created humankinds more than once and in a time long before the birth of genetics or a theory of natural selection, a classification scheme that has endured rock solid as a foundation for the study and understanding of human variation. With minor fluctuations, the idea that our species can be partitioned reasonably into four major groupings has withstood the Industrial and American Revolutions, the institution and dissolution of American slavery, the world wars, the rise of civil-right consciousness, the 20th-century explosion of modern biology, and even the new physical anthropology.

Is that an unfair characterization of contemporary anthropologists? When we enlightened, modern scientists now speak of geographical races or major racial groups or racial stocks, we are sharply aware that variation within any of these groups dwarfs interracial variability, that these groups represent only central tendencies, and that the boundaries between races are only approximations. Have not modern biological anthropologists especially, the experts on human variation, long abandoned the limitations of the 200-year-old four-fold scheme?

Before World War II, with a few exceptions, anthropologists in the United States and abroad not only accepted but also provided the scientific support for the traditional race categories. Like nearly all of their contemporaries, Hooton, Keith, and Hrdlicka presented human races as real, natural, and unquestioned varieties. In the decades following the war, there was a kind of intellectual cladogenesis, as the likes of Montagu, Washburn, Hiernaux, and Livingstone argued against the concept because of the complexity of variation and the discordance of traits. Michael Blakey (1987), by the way, has recently written that Franz Boas posed the powerful discordance argument against the typological race concept in 1931. And, while Ashley Montagu argued against the concept of race in the 1940s, the most active debates took place in anthropology in the 1960s when the non-race view of human variation began to gain significant support.

Since the 1970s, Liebermann, Reynolds, Littlefield, and some of their co-workers have studied physical anthropologists' view about race. At the 1987 meeting of the American Anthropological Association, Liebermann and his colleagues reported that only about 50 percent of the 147 physical anthropologists they surveyed in the United States agreed with the statement, "there are biological races within the species *Homo sapiens*" (Liebermann et al. 1987:8). The authors also mentioned that only about one in four cultural anthropologists agreed with the view that human races exist. The 1982 study by Littlefield, Liebermann, and Reynolds of the race position presented in textbooks is also interesting. In texts published between 1944 and 1979, 17 of 42 authors who commit to the question took the position that "races do not exist." Furthermore, they state:

> Although the no-race view was rarely expressed in physical anthropology texts before 1970, it had become the most frequent view by 1975–79, with only one quarter of the textbooks continuing to argue for the validity of the race concept. [Littlefield et al. 1982:646]

It has been suggested to me more than once, that discussing the race issue today is beating a dead horse, that the debaters of the 1960s dealt effectively with all of the significant issues. The odd thing about these comments is that they come from two kinds of anthropologists. One camp points to the successful demolition of the race concept, while the other claims that the existence of major races is so obvious that it is ludicrous to question.

Nonetheless, the question I raise here is how, in 1993, can it be that so many of us in our research, writing, and teaching accept in virtually its original form the four-fold scheme *invented* over 200 years ago. Linnaeus could not have understood the range and complexity of biological variation as it is known today. Not enough was known about the world. Nor could he have been aware of the complex array of mechanisms that affect biological variation. Nothing was known about evolutionary theory or genetics. No, if Linnaeus was correct in his characterization of the varieties of our species, he must have been incredibly lucky.

My personal brand of applied human biology is forensic anthropology. I, like others in my field, am regularly asked by the law enforcement or medical community to assist with the identification of decomposed human remains. Such identifications are normally a two-staged process. The initial stage is the construction of a biological profile—that is, a list of features, gleaned from the skeleton, that law enforcement personnel can compare to their missing-persons records. If a concordant missing person profile is located, then more specific information or data (such as dental records or X-rays) can be collected for an identification or exclusion comparison with the skeletal remains.

The categories that make up most such biological profiles are age at death, sex, stature, and race. In this publication, readers will be exposed to a range of techniques available for the estimation of race from a skeleton.

Probably the most frequently used metric method is one developed in 1962 by Giles and Elliot (1962). Through their studies of blacks and whites from the Terry collection and American Indians from Indian Knoll, Kentucky, they generated a series of discriminant function formulae that manipulate eight measurements of the skull. Their method requires two dichotomous tests: one to distinguish between blacks and whites, and another for American Indians and whites. In both tests, an individual's race is determined by whether or not a single score falls above or below a sectioning point. Using a modern forensic sample, Jantz and Moore-Jansen (1988) have published a revised set of values.

In addition to other metric techniques that are available, those provided by Howells (1970) and by Gill (1984) to name two, there are a number of nonmetric traits that are used for race determination. Krogman and Iscan in 1986 claimed:

> The more typically Negroid has undulating supraorbital ridges, sharp upper orbital margins, a rounded glabella, a plain frontonasal junction, and a wide interorbital distance. . . . White skulls have mesa-like supraorbital ridges, blunt upper orbital margins, a depressed glabella, "beetling" of the frontonasal junction and a narrow interorbital distance. [p. 272]

Dental observations, like shovel shaping among Asiatics and native Americans, are also routinely cited.

Again according to Krogman and Iscan, the accuracy of race estimation from the skeleton using traditional anthropological methods is quite high. They state: "On the basis of the usual morphological and morphometric studies, race can be determined from the skull in 85 to 90 percent of the cases" (1986:296). Ninety percent, by the way, is the level of accuracy cited by the same authors for *sex* determination from the skull.

One of the arguments voiced in favor of the race concept is that if races did not exist, then the biological differences used by forensic anthropologists to estimate race would not exist. As I have argued elsewhere (Sauer 1992), I disagree. Contrary to some of my colleagues, I do not believe that the traditional race concept is in any way vindicated by such forensic identification. The debate about race is whether or not the human species is divisible into a small number of naturally occurring groups. But consider the role of a forensic anthropologist in a human remains identification case. An individual's race is, along with age, sex, height, and date of disappearance, one of the descriptive features that regularly appears on a missing person report. Each time we guess correctly one of these categories on our skeletal remains report, we increase the likelihood of a match.

Is it conceivable that we would make an accurate assessment of the racial identity listed on a missing-person report, even if races did not exist?

Consider the possibility that human variation is systematic and continuous across a major geographic area, like Eurasia. And consider the possibility that there are no boundaries that separate this variation into a small number of groups. Is it not imaginable that with the appropriate methods of skeletal analysis we could identify the general area of origin along that continuum that is reflected in a set of skeletal remains? In fact, if that were true, we might be much better at identifying ancestry than is indicated by ascribing sweeping labels like white, black, or Asiatic. Unfortunately, such precision may be counterproductive. Because the labeling system used for missing persons in the United States is usually some variation of the traditional schemes, it makes sense to list one of those names on our anthropological reports. To provide an example, five options are provided by the National Crime Information Center's missing-persons report. They are: Asian, black, white, American Indian, and other (lucky Linnaeus!).

Several years ago, I was asked by a law enforcement official what I meant when I reported that a victim's ethnic identity was European/American. When I responded "white," he understood quite well. When we forensic anthropologists apply our analytical techniques to legal cases, it behooves us to report our data in a form that is most usable by the people we serve. If that means we must frame our results in outmoded terminology, then so be it. It is probably the best way to achieve the goal of identification. In ascribing a race name to a set of unidentified human skeletal remains, I contend that a forensic anthropologist is actually translating information about biological traits to the labeling system that is most likely to be available. Even if it were possible to estimate precisely from where in the world a victim's ancestor came from, what good would it do if a sheriff did not know where it was?

On the other hand, could forensic anthropologists contribute more effectively if they could identify ancestry with greater precision? The work of researchers like Howells (1973) and Brace and Hunt (1990) on human cranial variation suggests that we ought to be able to do better than estimate a major race. In fact, Brues suggests (1992) that we begin to focus on identifying populations rather than races. With sufficient flexibility in the choice of populations, she maintains, it may be reasonable to, in Alaska, distinguish between Eskimos and Aleuts, in California, among Chinese, Japanese, and Polynesians. She states:

> If we wish to get the greatest efficiency in forensic identification, we should stop trying to do it in a way in which the very real local variation becomes a mere static to confuse the results, and try to do it in a way in which local variation makes a positive contribution to a correct diagnosis. [Brues 1992:127]

I could not agree more. I find it quite interesting that so much of the research into the systematic variation in human skeletal form has been framed in the traditional race construct. In forensic anthropology there may be some rationale, but perhaps if we had treated the issue differently from the start, we might be farther ahead today.

My comments in this article have dealt with forensic anthropology alone. All of us, however, who deal with applied issues should appreciate the value of understanding public perceptions about what we do and about science in general. There are occasions when sensitivity to community perceptions about race may be quite useful. Soliciting the participation of subjects who are underrepresented in a community may require identifying certain groups—blacks or whites, for example. Perhaps there is value in presenting the results of applied research in terms that are most practical for and understood by the general public as well.

When we carry out research and attempt to *explain* human variation, however, I think it is paramount that we put racial categories aside, consider them as the folk taxonomies they are, and study human biological variation on its own terms. The clinal approach is one such strategy. At a lecture to research physicians at a Detroit hospital, I recently suggested that research into osteoporosis ignore the labels white and black and consider correlates of variation within races or without considering race as a primary variable. Most of those in attendance thought that was a silly suggestion—"Osteoporosis is a disease of whites." I hope the anthropological perspective is different.

## References Cited

Blakey, M. L.
1987 Skull Doctors: Intrinsic Social and Political Bias in the History of American Physical Anthropology. Critique of Anthropology 7:7–35.
Brace, C. L., and K. D. Hunt
1990 A Nonracial Craniofacial Perspective on Human Variation: A(ustralia) to Z(uni). American Journal of Physical Anthropology 82:341–360.
Brues, A.
1992 Forensic Diagnosis of Race—General Race vs. Specific Populations. Social Science and Medicine 34(2):125–128.
Giles, E., and O. Elliot
1962 Race Identification from Cranial Measurements. Journal of Forensic Sciences 7:147–157.
Gill, G. W.
1984 A Forensic Test for a New Method of Geographical Race Determination. *In* Human Identification: Case Studies in Forensic Anthropology. T. A. Rathbun and J. E. Buikstra, eds. Springfield, IL: Charles C Thomas.
Howells, W. W.
1970 Multivariate Analysis for the Identification of Race from Crania. *In* Personal Identification in Mass Disasters. T. D. Stewart, ed. Pp. 111–121. Washington, DC: American Museum of Natural History.
1973 Cranial Variation in Man. Cambridge, MA: Peabody Museum.
Jantz, R. L., and P. H. Moore-Jansen
1988 A Data Base for Forensic Anthropology: Structure, Content and Analysis. Report of Investigation No. 47. Department of Anthropology, University of Tennessee, Knoxville.
Krogman, W. M., and M. Y. Iscan
1986 The Human Skeleton in Forensic Medicine. Springfield, IL: Charles C Thomas.

Leiberman, L., et al.
1987 Informing the Public and the Disciplines about Human Variation: Obstacles and Alternatives. Paper presented at the 86th Annual Meeting of the American Anthropological Association, Chicago.

Linnaeus, C.
1757 Systema Naturae. Stockholm.

Littlefield, A., L. Lieberman, and L. Reynolds
1982 Redefining Race: The Potential Demise of a Concept in Physical Anthropology. Current Anthropology 23:641–655.

Sauer, N. J.
1992 Forensic Anthropology and the Concept of Race: If Races Don't Exist, Why Are Forensic Anthropologists so Good at Identifying Them? Social Science and Medicine 34(2):107–111.

# About the Contributors

*Nancy A. Bell* received her B.A. in anthropology from Emory University in 1990 and began work with Geo-centers, Inc., and the U.S. Army shortly thereafter. Her research has included pilot anthropometry, gender-integrated sizing of protective clothing and equipment, race and ethnic classification systems, and ethnic food prohibitions. Her career plans include graduate studies in cultural anthropology.

*Alice M. Brues* received her Ph.D. from Radcliffe in 1940. Afterward, she managed Earnest Hooton's osteology lab at Harvard and did applied anthropometry for the Army Air Force and Chemical Warfare Service during World War II. In 1946 she began teaching anatomy at the University of Oklahoma Medical School and conducted forensic investigations with the Oklahoma State Bureau of Investigation. Upon moving to the University of Colorado in 1965, Brues's research interests broadened to include morphology and evolution, as well as forensics. Highly active in her "retirement," Brues continues to inspire us all with the measure of clarity and common sense she brings to difficult research problems in bioanthropology.

*Claire C. Gordon* received her Ph.D. in bioanthropology from Northwestern University in 1982 and an M.S. degree in biostatistics from the Harvard University School of Public Health in 1990. Although initially trained in prehistoric human biology and mortuary archaeology, Gordon's interests shifted to contemporary populations when she came to Natick in 1983. During 1984–88, she planned and led a major anthropometric survey of the U.S. Army that included more than 132 body dimensions on 8,997 soldiers. Her research interests include gender and racial variation in morphometry, secular trends, statistical sizing methodology, and statistical simulation of human engineering and military logistics problems.

*Thomas M. Greiner* received his M.A. in anthropology from SUNY Binghamton in 1988. He began work with the U.S. Army shortly thereafter, digitizing hand photographs from the army's 1988 anthropometric survey. After completing a comprehensive volume on hand anthropometry, Greiner studied army secular trends and occupational differences in body size. In 1992 he returned to SUNY Binghamton to complete his doctoral thesis and to pursue his primary research interests in functional morphology and paleontology.

*Madeleine J. Hinkes* received her Ph.D. in anthropology from the University of Arizona in 1983. From 1985–92, she was on the scientific staff of the U.S. Army Central Identification Laboratory in Hawaii. Forensic investigations have taken her to Germany, Burma, Vietnam, Cambodia, the Marshall Islands, and Peru. Her research interests include human identification, biomechanics of trauma, and skeletal growth and development. In 1992 Hinkes joined Geo-Centers, Inc., to work with the U.S. Army on human engineering research for individual protective clothing and equipment.

*Stanley Rhine* received his Ph.D. from the University of Colorado in 1969. After four years at Colorado State University, he moved to the University of New Mexico in 1971. There he organized the Maxwell Museum's osteology collection and the university's graduate program in forensic anthropology. Rhine joined the staff of the New Mexico Office of the Medical Investigator in 1974 and has also held offices in the Anthropology Section of the American Academy of Forensic Sciences and on the American Board of Forensic Anthropology. In 1981 he helped to found the Mountain, Desert and Coastal Forensic Anthropologists, and served as co-editor of its 1990 publication, *Skeletal Attribution of Race.*

*Norman J. Sauer* received his Ph.D. in anthropology from Michigan State University in 1974, where he has been on the faculty since 1973 developing teaching and research programs in bioarchaeology and forensic anthropology. In 1984 Sauer published a definitive discussion of the role of physical anthropologists in death investigations (*Journal of Forensic Science* 29:1081–1086) and recently has considered difficulties in the various concepts of race used in evolutionary and forensic anthropology research (*Social Science and Medicine* 34). He is currently chair of the Physical Anthropology Section of the American Academy of Forensic Sciences.

*Kim S. Kimminau* received her Ph.D. in anthropology from Ohio State University in 1984, with primary research interests in dental enamel composition. As an assistant and later associate professor at Wichita State University, she taught courses in bioanthropology, osteology/odontology, and forensics. She began forensic work with the U.S. Army Central Identification Laboratory in January 1989 and was named its director in 1991. Kimminau's research interests are broad—including skeletal and dental biology, forensics, biostatistics, primate anatomy and behavior, and medical anthropology. She is particularly well known for her research on dietary and geographical variation in the compositional analysis of teeth. Kimminau's current research focuses on medical treatment effectiveness in Asian and Pacific Islander minority groups in Hawaii.

*Robert A. Walker* received his Ph.D. in anthropology from Kent State University in 1989. While completing his thesis, he served as field supervisor of the army's 1988 anthropometric survey and during the course of that study interviewed more than 26,000 soldiers regarding their race and ethnicity. Walker joined the teaching and research staff at Northwestern University Medical School in 1990 and then accepted his current position teaching anatomy at the New York Chiropractic College in 1992. His research interests include human variation and skeletal morphology.